Grandma's Sampler

Janie Eddleman

DEDICATION

For my children and grandchildren
with all my love.

CONTENTS

ACKNOWLEDGMENTS

To those who shared their stories and wisdom, thank you.

Thanks to Nancy O'Connell, who taught the writing classes I attended at Las Positas Community College, and introduced me to a Super Writing Group. I thank her and them for their encouragement, good advice and friendship.

Thanks to those who read these stories and essays, made suggestions for improvements and gave me the courage to put them together in this book.

.

INTRODUCTION

Everything in this book is true—from my point of view.

Truth is like a rainbow; how it looks depends on where you stand. The truth often depends on a person's past experiences, beliefs, hopes, fears, or faith in the storyteller. I recognize that someone in the same place at the same time probably would tell the story differently.

The title of this book, Grandma's Sampler, brings to mind both the samplers stitched by young women and the boxed candy samplers. The embroidered samplers were worked in various stitches as a specimen of skill, typically containing the alphabet and some mottoes. Likewise, I created this sampler book using a variety of styles and topics.

The first boxed candy that I can recall was Whitman's Sampler. The cover inside showed the locations of the candies. We chose candies by their name and description. Likewise, I hope that you'll use the table of contents to decide what to read. Sample the stories in any order—like we ate the candies.

The stories in this book were written for different reasons. A few were for a writing class. Sometimes I wrote to try to place myself in a situation to imagine how something happened. Other times, I am reporting a story that was told to me. In those cases, I tried to write it in the way I thought the reader would most likely understand the intent of the storyteller. Finally, some stories were written to add to this book.

Sometimes I changed the names of characters. It wasn't to protect anyone's reputation, because the characters in this book are honorable people.

In trying to capture the essence of a story, I sometimes created dialogue or even added characters, like the story about Uncle George.

Throughout the process of putting this book together, I have been haunted by a quote in *The Fact Checker's Bible: A Guide to Getting It Right.* Libel lawyer David Korzenik said, "Everyone thinks they've been misquoted. Most people would sue a mirror for what it shows them in the morning if they could." If you think you were misquoted, please accept my apologies. The truth does depend upon where one stands. In addition, memory plays tricks, especially if a story has been told many times.

I am thankful to live in a time when I am free to produce a book without intermediaries, like literary agents, publishers, or editors, and deliver it directly to you. On the other hand, I now have an appreciation of the added value those professionals give a book. I hope you'll read this book like a friend would— with a compassionate heart.

Ralph Waldo Emerson said, "Life is a succession of lessons which must be lived to be understood." Some of the lessons in this book were learned by me directly; others were given to me. I, in turn, pass them on to you.

TRUTH SEEKING

The right to search for truth
implies also a duty:
one must not conceal
any part of what
one has recognized to be true.

Albert Einstein

Self Portrait?

A question posed to me in Sweden took me nearly twenty years to answer.

"Do you know what makes this room's paintings different?" The smiling woman asked my sister Nita and me as we left a sunlit round room with floor to ceiling paintings.

Instead of being a fifty-one-year-old tourist wandering through a palace in Sweden, I felt like a sixth grader facing given a pop quiz. Besides that, I was tired and my feet hurt.

I didn't think it would be polite to tell her what I thought; *This room's so much more inviting than those other dim rectangular rooms with dark, gold-framed pictures hung in long lines.*

My sister and I were drawn to the light coming through the windows. We walked right past the pictures without looking at them. Who could resist that view with the cerulean sky and the quaint village hugging the lake?

We were fascinated by the perfectly round room with tall windows that didn't have any shutters or curtains. We both noticed and commented on the baby-cheek pink of the walls. Since the art wasn't protected from the sunlight, we thought the pictures were neither valuable nor important.

Fortunately, Nita has good manners. She politely asked, "Will you explain?"

The lady led us back into the room and waved toward the paintings. "These are all self-portraits. Don't you think that it's interesting to see what people want you to remember about them? Notice what they're wearing, who's with them, and what objects they include."

Instantly, the woman changed our attitude about the pictures.

Nita and I returned to the room. We didn't recognize any of the people depicted. Instead, we created characters based on the objects shown in their self-portraits. We lingered there a long time.

As we left the room Nita asked me, "What would you put in your portrait?"

I was flummoxed. One by one, I rejected the obvious replies. Nurses don't wear their nursing school's caps anymore. I don't have a symbol for any of my professions, so that's out. Anyway, who would recognize the meaning?

How could I show the importance of my family? And my friends? Their faces would be more like objects and wouldn't show my strong feelings I have for them.

I don't feel particularly attached to any place or any thing.

I do enjoy reading, travel and gardening, but that's not what I want to be remembered about me.

So, I continued to ponder Nita's question over the years.

Nita's query was similar to what I asked Mom when she was writing her memoir, "Mom, do you see any themes in your life? Threads that keep appearing again and again?"

Mom couldn't answer those questions. Eventually, I drafted the end notes for her memoir summarizing the themes of her life and why she had written her story. When I showed it to Mom, she said, "How did you know that? You wrote what I wish I had told you."

Finally, I've found my own answer. My self-portrait should have a rainbow in the background. I have spent a lifetime searching for the truth, the way others hunt for the pot of gold at the end of the rainbow. For me, truth is like a rainbow; how it looks depends on where you stand.

This book contains short stories or essays about some truths that I have accumulated. Sometimes truth came suddenly, like an epiphany. More often, I need to hear a truth repeatedly for me to finally grasp it. Occasionally, someone gave me a standard to live by that I would never have discovered on my own.

In summary, this book is about my life lessons.

Truth Is Like a Rainbow

Truth is like a rainbow; how it looks depends on where you stand.

When I see a rainbow overhead, I invariably search for the places where the ends rest. Fantasies of pots of gold still linger, even though I realize that each rainbow is a natural phenomenon. I understand that the sun has to be at my back and the rain in front of me for me to see a rainbow. I also know that I have to stand at exactly 42 degrees in relation to the sun's rays. Yet, knowledge of these facts doesn't diminish the emotional thrill that I have with each rainbow sighting.

Truth, on the other hand, isn't always thrilling. Sometimes it's as elusive as a pot of gold at the end of a rainbow.

I'd like to tell you about a time when truth depended on where I stood.

Truth telling is an important value in my family. So, when my high school's only science teacher Sister Suzanne introduced me to the scientific method and science projects, I felt like I had found my future.

How could I know that when Sister Suzanne handed me the application to the Indiana Girl Scientist contest that she was setting in motion another lesson from that taskmaster truth? I also didn't anticipate that this science project was also going to offer me another lesson in humility.

After Christmas vacation of my senior year, Sister Suzanne held out a large envelope, "Janet, I want you to fill out this application. You'll need to attach a science project report. You don't have to do a whole new project; you can use one of the ones that you have done in the past."

She made it sound simple, but I knew that my parents weren't comfortable with complicated forms. I wondered if this might be reaching too far beyond our little town in southern Indiana.

I looked around the science classroom, remembering the hours spent there. The classroom was in the basement of the 100-year-old building of the all-girls St. Rose Academy and showed that science was an afterthought. Situated by the furnace room, the forest green painted cement floor and white walls gave the room a sturdy feeling. A huge poster of the periodic table of elements covered one wall. We students sat at long tables which served as dissecting tables in biology class and lab stations in chemistry class. The equipment, like Bunsen burners, was limited, but not that many girls took science classes. A few old college textbooks stood on a shelf at the back at the room and served as reference books for the students.

Sister Suzanne thinks I can do this! I thought, storing the papers in my folder. *She's always finding new ways to push us. I doubt if I would have joined the Science Club if she hadn't suggested it. Or the Science Seminar. She wouldn't ask me to do anything that I'm not able to do.*

My body was sending me conflicting messages. My feet wanted to skip and my lips broke into a wide smile of pleasure. Yet, my gut churned with the thought of trying to fill out the forms and typing up that science report. (Copiers didn't exist yet.) My stomach had a sinking feeling, anticipating the rejection letter and how to handle that. Yet, my head considered possibilities.

Turning around at the doorway, I asked, "Which project do you think I should use?"

"The penicillin-resistant bacteria," Sister Suzanne replied.

Two months later, Sister Suzanne held out a piece of paper, "Janet, you're a finalist in the Indiana Girl Scientist!" I noticed a glimmer of a smile on her face as she watched me read the letter.

She looked at me and simply said, "Congratulations!" Then, almost as an afterthought, she added, "You're going to have to reproduce your science project and make a display. You can use test tubes from our supplies. Can you get the other supplies for your project—the penicillin, the Staphylococcus aureus bacteria and the culture medium—from the hospital again?"

A little over two years before, our landlord Dr. Ewing had asked the pathologist at Good Samaritan Hospital's laboratory to help me with a science project. For the next two Saturday mornings, I went to the hospital with Dr. Ewing. While Dr. Ewing made rounds, I visited the laboratory, "getting an idea of the kind of work we do," as the pathologist said.

A young technician Judy Ruppel took me under her wing. Her spotless white lab coat could have made her appear severe, but her short naturally curly hair and gap-toothed smile telegraphed Judy's friendly ways. While she did her routine work, she explained the purpose of the various tests and how the equipment worked. She must have noticed my eyes widen with wonder when she took a stack of Petri dishes out of the warmer.

The Bacteriology Lab was all angles and hard surfaces. Overhead fluorescent lights and the under-cabinet lights hovering above the work surface shined brighter than the sunlight streaming in the window. The smell of the phenol that Judy used to disinfect the counters hung in the air. The hollow sound of the dishes being set on the table reverberated in the room.

Could this be like Sister Suzanne's bacteriology book? I wondered. I recalled devouring the yellowed pages of the reference book from the science classroom. I envied Judy getting to do the things that were described in the book.

My eyes widened as Judy held up a Petri dish with bright red medium that had three round creamy-golden colonies of bacteria growing on it.

Holding the dish for me to see, Judy said, "These are growths of *Staphylococcus aureus*."

Another dish had a growth of *Staph aureus* surrounding and touching a little paper saturated with penicillin. "Those are resistant to penicillin," Judy explained.

The golden growths looked just like the description in the bacteriology book. The concepts that had enthralled me were Judy's everyday work. This was like a dream come true, my pot of gold at the end of the rainbow!

I was hooked! I wanted to do a science project that involved bacteriology. Was it possible?

Dr. Ewing walked into the room. "Janet, what do you think of our laboratory?"

Before I could answer, the pathologist said, "When you come back next week, we'll put our heads together and see if we can come up with a project for you. Which area of our lab did you find most interesting?"

The word slipped out of my mouth before my brain could think it over, "Bacteriology." Then, hesitantly, I added, "Maybe using *Staph aureus*?"

The following Saturday at the end of our time together, the pathologist said, "Let's go over these supplies again. Just to be sure you have everything you need."

He named the items, touching each one, as if the tap of his finger put a check on his internal list. "*Staph aureus* culture. Test tubes. Agar for culture medium. Pipette. Better give you two, just in case one breaks. Penicillin solution. Phenol.

"Judy did a good job teaching you to use a pipette and how to make sterile media. Now, when you get home, you need to build an incubator. Cardboard's a good insulator. You can use a light bulb with a blinker and adjust the temperature by making holes in the box.

"Good luck."

When I left the hospital that day with the box of supplies, I envisioned myself producing penicillin-resistant bacteria. The project was based upon the survival of the fittest. Theoretically, if the bacteria were introduced to a very weak concentration of penicillin, some of them might survive and produce offspring which were also unaffected by a similar level of penicillin. Incubating some of those bacteria in a slightly stronger solution of penicillin would again kill the weak, but the fit would survive to be exposed to increasingly strong solutions.

Each morning I checked the test tubes inoculated with the bacteria the day before and found the medium was cloudy. The bacteria were thriving, showing that they were resistant to the penicillin solutions!

Those bacteria won me the First Place at St. Rose Academy's Science Fair and entry to the regional science fair. In a way, that prize also led to my meeting my future husband Jim, who delivered my first lesson in humility from this science project.

Today not many couples can say that their mothers arranged their first meeting. To our mothers, who had been classmates in grade school, their carpooling scheme seemed like a way for two childhood friends to save each other a hundred mile drive.

My friend Ann Eddleman and I were both entitled to go to the Science Fair in Evansville. Her mother had agreed to take us and our projects to the fair. On the last day of the fair, Mom and Dad would take Ann and me to see the other projects and bring our displays home.

That trip was memorable for at least two reasons, the people in the car and Jim's comment about my science project.

When the car arrived at our house, there were already four people in it. Ann introduced me to her mother, her uncle Vincent and her brother Jim. When my display and report were loaded into the car, sixteen-year-old Jim got in the driver's seat and his uncle was in the front passenger seat. Ann, her mother and I sat in back.

It takes at least an hour to drive to Evansville, but I don't remember anything about the drive there. Those memories were erased by Jim's comment when we took our displays out of the car.

"Did you know you spelled milliliter wrong?" Jim asked.

I looked at him in disbelief. "I know it's right," I replied. "No one mentioned a misspelling at the Science Fair. Sister Suzanne would have noticed it and told me." Then, a little less assured, I continued, "Wouldn't the judges have commented on it?" I desperately thought to myself, *It has to be correct!*

I was proud of the display. It had taken me hours to hand-print all the letters. I had practiced using the perfect-sized nib on a pen dipped in India ink until I become sure-handed enough to draw perfectly straight identical letters. Doing the project and writing the report had been less challenging than constructing the pegboard display for the test tubes and hand lettering the description of the project and its results. Ann's big brother cast a shadow of doubt on my high hopes for the Regional Fair.

All the way home, I pictured myself looking in the dictionary and finding the correct spelling was "m-i-l-l-e-l-i-t-e-r."

Jim and his uncle Vincent talked most of the way home. At times, those of us in back listened or joined in their conversation. When Jim told a joke that had some bathroom language, I was surprised at the hearty laughter and lack of disapproval from the others. I thought, *This family's different. I bet they laugh a lot at home.*

To my chagrin, that evening I found an unpleasant truth in the dictionary. Milliliter is not spelled "milleliter."

At the end of that day, I knew that Ann's good-looking older brother was a better speller than I, smart, old enough to drive and bold. Mostly, I thought about the numerous times the misspelled "milleliter" appeared on the display and in the accompanying report. The prolonged dread of returning to Evansville began.

Fortunately, the science fair wasn't a spelling contest. The judges had not based their decision on spelling. An Honorable Mention was on my display!

It's hard to believe that the results of a science project for Indiana Girl Scientist were even more humiliating than my misspelling of milliliter.

"The bacteria aren't growing in penicillin," I informed Sister Suzanne. "If I put some of the Staph culture in a test tube without penicillin, the medium gets cloudy within 24 hours. But if I put it in a test tube that contains any penicillin at all, nothing happens."

I held back the tears trying to well up in my eyes.

"Why do you think that is?" Sister Suzanne asked.

Oh, no! She wants me to think scientifically, I thought. The shame and panic subsided as I reported my deductions.

15

"The incubator temperature has been stable, so I can rule that out. So far, I can only think of two other possible reasons for the problem. First, the bacteria I got from the hospital lab are from a different colony and maybe they don't have the hardiness to become resistant. Second, although I don't think it's possible, perhaps I made a mistake in calculating the strength of the penicillin solution.

"I can begin by making another penicillin solution, making sure the strengths are correct. Then, if the bacteria still won't grow, I'll go back to the lab and ask for another Staph aureus specimen. That's all that I can think of doing."

Even after taking both of those steps, the cultures that contained penicillin never became cloudy.

I reported back to Sister Suzanne, "I don't know what to do. How can I go to Indianapolis with no results?"

Sister Suzanne sighed, "Science is about having reproducible results. Write your report and include all three experiences—the two exercises done two years ago and this last series of experiments. You'll have to take the project to Indianapolis as it is."

My humiliation was nearly overwhelming as I rode with my parents and Sister Suzanne and with those clear lifeless tubes to the state capitol. I dreaded being compared to the nine other girl finalists. Sister Suzanne had told me that I was the only one from a small school; the others all came from big schools. One of them was the daughter of an Indianapolis science teacher whose students often won science contests. Reminding myself that being at the contest was an honor in itself didn't make me feel any better.

When I saw the professional quality of the other exhibits, my sense of humiliation was almost unendurable.

During the interview with the panel of science teachers and professionals, I calmly explained my theory. I answered questions about my project, including ones about the discrepancies between the three experiments. Describing the scientific process was easy, but I had no explanation for the failure of the bacteria to thrive this last time. I reviewed the steps I took in trying to replicate my earlier success. The panel also asked questions about my family, how I had gained access to the bacteria and penicillin, other science projects that I had done, and my future plans.

With a heavy heart, I went with Mom, Dad and Sister Suzanne to the awards ceremony. The second runner-up and runner-up were announced. Then I heard the emcee say, "This year's Indiana Girl Scientist is Janet Holscher." No one was more surprised than I!

When we were driving home, I asked Sister Suzanne, "How could I have gotten this award when my science project was such a failure?"

She answered, "Your project had good logic. It had worked twice before. But I think the real difference was that you told the truth. Science is about truth. You behaved like a scientist faithfully reporting the facts, whether they were convenient or not."

That day I grasped the importance of truth telling...and I had been awarded the impossible pot of gold at the end of the rainbow!

Years later, while working as a nurse in an Intensive Care Unit, I found the explanation for why the bacteria didn't grow for the Indiana Girl Scientist project. I was reading literature trying to understand the many types of penicillin and I stumbled onto the fact that aqueous penicillin needs refrigeration. Without refrigeration the efficacy of aqueous penicillin is destroyed, whereas crystalline penicillin does not require protection from heat.

This newfound knowledge finally clarified the puzzling results of that science project; the truth shifted with this new point of view. In my science projects, I had never grown drug-resistant bacteria! Instead, during the first set of experiments using solutions of aqueous penicillin, I had merely demonstrated the inefficacy of that particular form of penicillin in temperatures equivalent to my incubator.

I was finally standing in the right place to see the truth of my science project.

Truth is like a rainbow; how it looks depends on where you stand. No two people can even see the same rainbow, because the effect is dependent on the line of sight. I'm the only one who saw the truth of my science project and it took seven years for me to be standing in the right place.

Santa Secrets

"Mom, I've been thinking. I don't believe that there's a Santa," declared my four-year-old son Danny.

I held the dish I was washing above the soapy water. "What makes you say that?"

"When I looked up our chimney, I saw that it was so small that even a skinny person could not get down it. And Santa's fat. Anyway, lots of kids live in places that don't have a chimney."

Danny listed his findings so fast that I couldn't interrupt. "Then I thought about all the Christmas presents that Santa Claus is supposed to deliver. He can't possibly get to everybody's home in one night."

Danny took a breath, smiled and continued. "If Santa parked his sleigh on our roof, I'd hear the reindeer stamping up there. Besides, I don't believe reindeer can fly."

How could I refute his reasoning? So, I told him the truth. "You're right. BUT, almost all of the children who are your age believe in Santa. You can't tell them that Santa isn't real. That's for parents to tell. Do you understand?"

Danny nodded and went off to think some more.

Two days later, Danny returned with more findings. "There's no Easter Bunny, and there's no Tooth Fairy either."

"You're right again." I said sadly, because our home had lost its last believer in fairy tales.

Danny kept his promise not to tell the Santa secret to any other children.

Unlike Danny, I never questioned whether Santa was real. I was a perfect example of the Sophocles quote, "What people believe prevails over the truth."

One morning in the December of my eighth year, I sat on the cold cement steps at Sacred Heart School, playing Jacks with my third grade classmates. We were quietly talking as we took turns using the big smooth porch by the front door of school for our playing surface. My classmates were talking about Christmas and what they wanted.

"There's no Santa," my cousin Kathryn, who was a fourth grader, casually mentioned. The other kids nodded in agreement, but not me.

Someone noticed and said to me, "You believe in Santa!?"

There was no doubt in my voice, as I firmly replied, "Yes."

"Your mother hasn't told you?" my friends Andrea and Sharon asked.

Told me what? I thought to myself. The puzzled look must have betrayed my thoughts.

"That there's no Santa," finished Kathryn.

I innocently replied, "He's real." I pictured the man with the rubber mask and cotton beard who wore a red flannel suit with white cotton trim. I explained, "His helper comes to our house on Christmas Eve. The real Santa can't see everyone, but he has helpers and they're all wearing Santa outfits." Even my friends laughed.

Kathryn declared, "If you don't believe us, ask your mother."

That afternoon, I started to tell Mom about the incident. Before I finished the first sentence, she whisked me off to her bedroom and closed the door.

"Did you talk about this to anyone else?" Mom asked.

"No," I replied.

Mom stooped next to me. "I wondered when you would figure it out. Your Aunt Marguerite said I should tell you—that you're getting too old." Looking into my eyes, she asked, "Do you really believe in Santa?"

"Yes," I whispered to my toes.

"Janet, there's no Santa Claus," she said.

How could that be? I wondered. *I had seen his helper with my own eyes! Everyone, including Mom, had. How could Santa not be real?*

I approached this quandary logically. "But his helper comes to Grandma Holscher's Christmas party. And he finds us wherever we live each year on Christmas Eve," I argued.

Mom touched my arm softly. "That's Uncle Ray. He dresses up in an outfit Grandma made."

"But how does Uncle Ray get all the gifts to give us each year?" I asked, trying to hold on to my version of the truth.

"Each year after dark, either your dad or I put the toys on the front porch. When Uncle Ray arrives, he just starts bringing them in."

I visualized past Christmases. Santa's helper carried in a big white bag overflowing with gifts to Grandma's parties. Aunt Betty and Aunt Mary read the names on the gifts for Santa to distribute. Some of the gifts were ones we had purchased for the people whose name we had drawn a few weeks prior to the party. Santa was like a mailman at that party.

On Christmas Eve at our home, Santa had a few gifts in his bag, but he kept going outside to get more gifts. I imagined that they came from his sleigh, although his reindeer were very quiet. I began to understand that I had been so captivated by the gifts that I had not considered the logistics of their delivery.

The Christmas when we lived near Bruceville, when I was in the first grade, flickered to life. I recalled Mom and Dad pulling the curtain back and looking out the window for Santa. They said that they were worried that the snow was going to stop Santa's car, while I wondered at their ignorance. Instead of looking for car lights, they should have been listening for sleigh bells! Didn't they realize that Santa's sleigh and magical reindeer could get through any kind of weather? I knew that Santa's helper would be the one to carry our presents into the house. He never failed to come before we went to bed.

That year Mom and Dad discussed whether to keep us up to see Santa. Mom was worried about us being tired the next day at Grandma's. Mom said something about being last on Santa's list because we lived in Bruceville.

Santa finally did arrive. We didn't hear a car; we did hear sleigh bells outside the door.

He seemed really happy to get the bottle of Mogan David wine that Mom gave him when he left. When he was gone, Mom told Dad that maybe that wasn't a good gift for Santa.

At the time, I imagined that the big heavy bottle would weigh his sleigh down. I knew he was going to share it with the elves, because it was much too big for one man to drink. Today, I realize that Mom thought that Uncle Ray had received similar gifts from my aunts and uncles on his route, and he may have already been enjoying them.

Closeted in the bedroom with Mom, it seemed like I was underwater trying to hear her words. She was saying something about how much harder it was this year. She was saying that she knew she had to tell me about Santa before this Christmas. Then I heard her clearly.

"We don't have much money this year. Now that you know there's no Santa Claus, you won't get any toys this Christmas Eve. But I did buy some material to make you a new skirt for Christmas. You can't tell any children that there's no Santa. It was wrong of Kathryn to tell you."

Mom reached under her bed and retrieved a paper sack.

"I've made this skirt for you and I need to measure its length, so I can hem it."

I let Mom put the skirt on me.

I had to stand still in a circular skirt made of corduroy. While Mom marked the hem, I made myself look at the bright aqua fabric with a navy wavy pattern. I hated that shade of blue and the fabric was too stiff to drape softly, like my friends' skirts.

I was fence post stiff. Although I wanted to cry, no telling emotion rose on my face.

I thought, *Santa's gone. I won't be getting any gifts. But all of the younger kids will.* I imagined Christmas Day at Grandma and Grandpa Holscher's wearing this skirt and not carrying a toy. I would be the only child there without a favorite Christmas gift to show off, looking like the naughty child who had been crossed off Santa's list.

A tornado tore my world apart and scattered my illusions. I didn't say anything and Mom probably thought I was sorting the Santa fantasy into a new reality. In a way, I was, but she had no idea of how barren the new truth was for me.

The pain was compounded by having to keep *the secret*. I had promised not to tell any other children about Santa. Not being sure who did know kept me quiet. I never exposed the secret or my sense of loss.

I've wondered why I didn't tell Mom how I felt that day. I'd like to believe that, even at that tender age, I felt Mother's overwhelming sadness. She did have tears in her eyes when she told me I wouldn't get any playthings.

My not having a favorite Christmas toy to take to Grandma and Grandpa's may have been harder for Mom and Dad than me. Later, knowing the source of the gifts, I began to understand that the toys brought to play with our cousins, also were an indicator of parents' ability to make the purchases. How humiliating that year must have been for Mom and Dad.

It's a shame that I didn't express my true feelings that afternoon, or as soon as I had sorted them out, because I believe Mom and Dad would have found a way to give me a token toy. Instead I learned a pattern of behavior that I repeated until I was twenty years old when I found a voice to speak up for what I really wanted—to marry Jim. But that's another story.

There is a saying, "All things come around." In my fifties, my favorite color palette began to move from floral pinks and blues to lilac and soft teals. If I were to see the material that Mom used for my skirt now, I would be drawn to it. How could she see the spirit that has taken so long to unfold?

I still hate corduroy!

Watching Mobiles

Sometimes I feel like a caged mobile.

Longing to dance,

    to freely express my thoughts,

        feelings,

            wishes,

                dreams,

    to share them,

        react to the responses.

I want to release the encrusted mechanism,

    to spring into action

    leaping beyond the

        boundaries of my being

        into a world of new visions.

A myriad of one-inch white paper circles gently swayed in response to passersby, who were only an arm's length away from them. The precise and intricate ballet was choreographed years before by Alexander Calder. Gray shadows glided past and through one another. Calder's mobile *Universe* danced before our eyes. My friend Cheryl sighed, "A-a-h. This is an example of a talented curator breathing life into a piece of art."

Her comment resonated with me. That night as I drifted off to sleep, I recalled works by Calder and lined them up on a continuum from free interaction with the environment to frozen stiffness. Could the presentation of the works tell me more about the curators and their institutions than about Calder's imagination?

Alexander Calder is one of my favorite artists. He is the father of the mobile. He used his engineering background to balance massive and complex structures from one point. I read that Calder had the idea for mobiles while visiting his friend Piet Mondrian's studio in Paris. Calder playfully suggested that Mondrian cut up one of his canvases and suspend the distinctive, brightly colored geometric figures separately; an idea that Mondrian rejected. Intrigued with the concept of art moving and floating in the air, Calder returned to his own studio, cut shapes from colored papers, suspended them, and combined them to create his first mobile.

Through mobiles, Calder extended his art beyond the boundaries of the physical objects that make up mobiles. The space they move in becomes part of the artwork, interacting with light and air currents. When his small mobiles echo the vibrations of nearby visitors with delicate stirrings of their own, they seem to be drawing in space. More exciting, with proper lighting, shadows of his art leap on to surrounding objects and walls.

I first fell in love with Calder's work in Paris in the fall of 1996. If Jim's illness hadn't slowed us down, maybe I would have continued to look only at the objects floating in space. But that day, Jim and I sat in the middle of a large quiet room filled with Calder mobiles and waited for him to catch his breath. The carefully-designed subdued lighting of the exhibition prompted me to look beyond the materials of colored paper, wires, and metal pieces. Each mobile moved to its own inner rhythm and sent its shadows gliding across the walls, like graceful ice skaters on a moonlit night. I felt like I was watching a cosmic ballet.

A year later, I rushed to the Calder works on display at San Francisco's Museum of Modern Art (SF MOMA). I was anxious to see the Calder ballet again.

I found tiny exquisitely balanced metal objects floating but incarcerated in a lucite box barred from human interaction.

A groan growled inside me, *Where is the Calder magic? It's trapped, like specimens on a pathologist's slides, sterilized and frozen. Those bright lights are even stripping them of shadow play!*

The mobile poised heavily before me, reduced to a skeleton, unable to dance or play; its magic dissipated. Although I was looking at Calder's shapes and lines, the mobile was entombed, deadened and unable to respond to human presence. My heart was heavy; my eyes filled with tears.

A month later, I hesitantly entered the Calder exhibit that the San Jose Museum of Art had organized with the Whitney Museum of American Art. I inhaled sharply. Sandy Calder's playful spirit had been released! His mobiles spun and twirled in slow motion and a whole ensemble of shadows pranced and cavorted on a bright red wall.

Calder's works seemed lighthearted and free, inviting Cheryl and me and the other museum goers to enjoy them. Even the stabiles seemed alive, beckoning us to notice the roundness and fullness of a simple spiral's shadows playing on the white wall. Once again, the grace of Calder's mobiles was showcased.

A tiny acrobatic shape balanced on a nail just a breath away from me. It wasn't my fingers that itched to touch the piece; it was my breath. I pursed my lips and exhaled gently. The acrobat responded and jerked to life. The man of steel rode my air. He twisted and twirled on his nail, filling the space as Calder had intended, then he jumped to the wall behind, propelled by the curator's lighting.

Later, Cheryl and I circled around to the beginning of the exhibit to watch the tiny white circles of the Universe weaving, twisting and flowing in space again. Its rhythms were replies to the currents stirred by the passersby. Anchored from above, Universe was like an upside-down kelp bed, eternally rising, falling, and swaying slowly in unison, reacting to each incoming wave.

Universe's sense of order filled the museum space. The shapes danced past each other, almost touched, then backed away, held deliciously close by the creator's design, yet never becoming entangled. They mimicked a school of fish, reflecting the bent rays of sun, individuality replaced by group action, dancing as one, swooping and swirling.

Standing there, I told Cheryl about the difference between the Calders I had seen in Paris and at SF MOMA. "I'm relieved that the Calder magic I saw in Paris was not my imagination."

"Just remember that a good curator released Calder's magic," she responded.

Since that night in San Jose, I search for and recall the locations of Calder works, the way I do ice cream shops.

There is a massive black Calder stabile and mobile in the central atrium of the United States Senate's Hart Office Building. Standing at a foot of the thirty-nine ton stabile *Mountains*, I wondered what the architect or interior designers were thinking when they crammed it in there. Visitors are dwarfed. The mobile *Clouds* is suspended above. Its movement is supposed to be controlled by a computerized motor, but it seems as unmoving as the *Mountains* below. When citizens visit their senator, I suspect that the trapped art works communicate a message about the size and immobility of our government. Or maybe, the black cloud hanging over us is a reminder that Calder came to Washington on November 10, 1976 to make the final adjustments to his model, and died later that evening after returning to New York.

Fortunately, most of Calder's works retain his playfulness, love of dance, especially ballet, interest in color and show off his exquisite sense of balance. Gombrich wrote that Calder "longed for art to reflect the mathematical laws of the universe, but for him such an art could not be rigid and static. The universe is in constant motion but held together by mysterious balancing forces, and it was this idea of balance that first inspired Calder to construct his mobiles."[1] His concept was so successful that, once demonstrated, it was translated into a "toy." Few of us think of the universe when we see a Calder mobile, but we do feel its orderliness and balance.

Calder's works speak to me, urging me to look beyond the shapes, colors, and movement before me, to watch its response to its surroundings and to see how far its influence stretches. Through them, I am learning to use curator eyes to take second and third stretching looks at other art, as well as at history, cultures, and my own life.

> Where is the curator that sees
>
> beyond my bones and skin?
>
> Who releases the borders of my life
>
> to meander, interweave with
>
> dreams and visions of my elders?

---

[1] Gombrich, E.H. The Story of Art. 16th edition. New York: Phaidon Press Inc. 2002. p. 584.

GLIMPSES ACROSS THE THRESHOLD

Because I have a body
  I experience the world
  through my senses.

Some people can see across the threshold
  to other worlds

I thank them
  for telling me
  about those moments.

May these true stories
  expand your Truth.

Can a Memory Be Lost?

The long drawn out "P-sh-ist" of the ventilator was the first sound I heard when I entered the Coronary Care Unit (CCU) one morning at the beginning of my shift. A hose from the steamer-trunk-sized piece of equipment was attached to a tube in the mouth of an unconscious plump blonde-haired woman.

My heart sank when I saw my co-worker Dorothy. The night nurse's characteristic light-hearted greeting was smothered in a puckered up sourness. I stiffened, because I knew that Dorothy's mood was a reliable indicator of how the day would go.

"It's not right," Dorothy muttered. "Look at her. Fifty-three years old. Heart attack and unconscious God knows how long. She's a vegetable. It's cruel. I wished all night long that I would happen to trip on the electric cord and stop this nonsense."

I blanketed my concern in nursing tasks. I checked the woman's blood circulation by pressing down on her fingernail, noticing how the hurried removal of her bright red nail polish had marred an otherwise perfectly manicured hand. The blanched nail quickly returned to its pink color.

Good circulation and oxygenation, I thought. *The ventilator's doing its job.* I tried not to think about this woman's future.

Yet, a procession of the images of the numerous patients with heart attacks that I had cared for in the Coronary Care Unit (CCU) came to mind. They all looked so stripped down and helpless during their time here with their kingdoms reduced to the size of a mattress and their regalia replaced by a gown that left their backsides exposed. In the 1970s, every heart attack patient faced the possibility of impending death.[2] Each of them was wired to monitors that signaled any deadly heart arrhythmias and also tattled any large body movements. They also had a tube running from a bottle of intravenous solution to a needle in the hand, ready to carry life-saving drugs. They endured this lack of privacy and constant watching for at least three days, because they were constantly reminded that an arrhythmia might kill them. Their eyes almost always revealed deep-seated regret. In facing the possibility of dying, heart attack patients almost obsessively reviewed their life and judged whether it was lived well.

I shuddered and looked at the woman's closed eyes. *If she could speak, what would she say?*

Returning to the nurses' desk, I touched Dorothy's shoulder and asked, "Hard night? Do you need help with anything before report?"

Dorothy's pen stopped. "Not really. I can do this after report."

Two other nurses and I followed Dorothy into the Nurses' Lounge for the change-of-shift report. Dorothy pulled her notes out of her uniform pocket. "The woman in Bed A is a fifty-three year old female named Barbara Long, who had a massive heart attack. She was found unconscious in her home yesterday evening. The family started CPR. The ambulance crew

---

[2] This was before lifesaving angioplasty, stents, and coronary bypass surgery established blood flow before heart tissue was damaged.

continued trying to resuscitate her the entire twenty minutes from her house to here. They intubated her in ER. She has been here since 9:00 p.m. last night.

"She does respond to pain, but nothing else. She hasn't had any arrhythmias here in CCU.

"One last comment," Dorothy said, pausing to emphasize her point and looking directly into the eyes of each of the nurses in the room. "Don't do this to me! I'm her age and I wouldn't want to be stuck like this for the rest of my life."

The other nurses clucked and nodded their heads.

I was relieved that Mrs. Long wasn't assigned to me, but I helped the other nurses move the oversized woman and kept an eye on her monitor. I helped Margaret, Mrs. Long's evening nurse, reposition her one last time before leaving.

The next morning, I approached CCU with a shadow of dread straggling behind me. I opened the door, but the ventilator's rhythmic noise was missing.

Oh, no, I thought. *Mrs. Long died.*

The curtains were drawn around Bed A.

Wonder who's in that bed now? Can't be as bad as yesterday.

Dorothy's hand slipped out from behind the curtain and opened it wide. The bed was in an upright position and a woman was brushing her teeth.

Dorothy flashed a smile at me and said, "Barbara, this is Janie. She's one of the nurses who took care of you yesterday.

"Janie, since you're a few minutes early, would you mind helping me change this bed? Barbara's been awake for about a half hour and I had time to give her a bath. By the time we're done with the bed, the others'll be here, and we can go into report. I have a story to tell you."

Dorothy's sparkle had returned, but she usually had jokes to tell, not stories.

In report, Dorothy said, "Before we start, I have to tell you what Margaret told me when I came on shift last night.

About seven o'clock yesterday evening, the ventilator alarm went off. Margaret rushed to the bedside to see Mrs. Long holding the ET tube in her hand; Mrs. Long was breathing on her own. Margaret said that you could have knocked her over with a feather, because the woman hadn't shown any signs of waking up earlier.

Mrs. Long asked Margaret, "Where am I?"

Margaret turned the ventilator off and told Mrs. Long, "You're in the hospital. You've had a heart attack."

Mrs. Long seemed to consider what Margaret had said, but she still looked puzzled. "I came here in an ambulance, didn't I?"

Margaret nodded and put the ends of her stethoscope in her ears and prepared to listen to her patient's lungs and heart.

Mrs. Long touched Margaret's hand. "I remember that my father and brother were with me in the ambulance. Dad held my hand and Mark stood at my feet. At first, they scared me, but they told me that it wasn't my time yet and that I was going to be okay."

Margaret responded, "That's unusual. I've never heard of family being allowed to ride along in the ambulance before."

Mrs. Long searched Margaret's eyes and said, "You don't understand. They've been dead for years. That's what scared me at first."

Dorothy wasn't finished. She looked directly at her audience and continued, "Here's the funny part. Margaret mentioned the ambulance ride to Mrs. Long a couple of hours later and the woman didn't remember anything about it!"

Dorothy motioned everyone closer with her hand and in a secretive tone continued, "Margaret told me that she was more spooked by Mrs. Long losing the memory than her story about her father and brother being with her. She asked me to tell you about this incident. What do you think is the truth? Could Mrs. Long's story been true? If so, how could she forget so quickly?"

No one answered Dorothy's questions, but they all thought about them.

Mrs. Long's recovery was without incident and she returned to her job three months after being released from the hospital. She retired fifteen years later. She never remembered what she had told a nurse about her ambulance ride.

This incident was the first time I heard about a person being visited by dead family members and friends when they were close to death. My ideas about the connections with people who have died were stretched. While working with hospice patients, seeing deceased loved ones became normal and was considered to be a sign that death is approaching.

I wish I had asked Dorothy if she changed her mind about being put on a ventilator after what happened to Mrs. Long.

I learned that the healthcare decisions of others depend on where they have stood.

Could we have experienced miracles like Mrs. Long's and forgotten them?

Can Dreams Come True?

What smells so good? Ed sniffed. *Food? I don't think I've ever eaten anything with this aroma.*

He followed his nose and found a tiny kitchen area. That's it! The food was warm – ready to eat.

He tasted the rice.

Hmmm! Delicious. Vegetables. Crunchy. Sort of sweet with…

He rolled the food around in his mouth.

A hint of vinegar. Foreign food. Chinese?

Ed looked around and saw some packages with characters on them.

Asian, for sure, he thought.

Where am I? Ed wondered. *How can anyone cook in this miniature space? If I stretch my arms out, I can touch both sides of the …. What is this?*

Why isn't anyone here? The food's warm. Those dishes and trays are tiny! Where am I? It feels <u>so</u> foreign here.

This isn't a room. It's the tail of an airplane! But there aren't any passengers up front.

It's broken off!

Ed looked out of the broken fuselage.

How can this be? There are parts of the plane scattered everywhere out there! The seats look like toys that had been dropped from the sky.

They're lying on their sides, upright and upside down. People are still strapped in some of them.

A feeling of dread began to tug at his stomach. He walked among the seats. A woman dressed like a stewardess lay on the ground. He bent down and touched her face.

It's still warm, but she's not breathing. No pulse either. What am I doing here? These people are _all_ dead. I just tasted the food that they were going to eat. I wouldn't have done that if I had known about this.

Ed's stomach began to ache.

Where am I? This is horrible. I shouldn't be here. This is like walking inside a movie. It's all wrong. I don't belong here.

A bit of yellow flickered to his right. He faced it. The whole side of the mountain glimmered. His eyes focused and he saw a mass of shimmering yellow leaves.

If I didn't know better, I'd say that I'm in Colorado.

A sunbeam reflected off a piece of white fuselage near Ed. He stepped back.

Japanese Air Lines, Ed said to himself.

His knees trembled. *Did I say that to myself? Or did someone else say it?*

Ed set up with a jerk. He was sweating and he had that dreaded feeling deep in his gut. Now he knew where he was, but he didn't know where he'd been. Feelings of dread and fear burbled up and nearly paralyzed him.

"Barbara! Wake up! It's happened again." He touched her shoulder and whimpered. "Barbara, please, please wake up. I need you."

Barbara turned her face with her eyes still closed toward Ed's voice. If he hadn't been so upset, he would have seen the childlike peace in her lidded eyes and Mona Lisa smile. Her lips tightened and her eyelids twittered. "Wh-a-t?" She rolled toward Ed.

"I had another one of those dreams. It's bad this time."

"Ed?" she mumbled.

"I dreamed of a plane crash. In Colorado, I think. I just don't know when it's gonna happen."

Barbara's eyelids opened halfway, but her eyes remained unfocused.

Ed told Barbara about his dream, about tasting the food, about touching the dead woman, about the plane parts and bodies scattered over the hillside and about the quivering aspens. He didn't care that she wasn't quite awake. He needed to pour the words out.

"What a dream!" Barbara mumbled from her haze. She coaxed him down beside her and held him close.

"Maybe if we go back to sleep, you can dream a better ending?"

She fell asleep hugging him to her, but Ed stared into space. His gut tingled and hurt.

The next morning, Ed walked into the kitchen in a haze unaware of the aroma of frying bacon and barely noticing his four children seated at the table eating breakfast. When he stood beside Barbara, who was producing the soothing smells of bacon and coffee, he could feel her confident strength. His drooping shoulders slowly straightened, but the sense of dread still nibbled at his psyche.

"That dream. It's still with me. I can't figure out what to do," he said in low tones, so that only Barbara heard him.

"We'll talk after the kids leave for school." She handed him a plate with an egg and bacon on it. "Try to eat some breakfast."

He sat down and ate. The smells, tastes, and the empty chatter at the table could not break through the bubble of the dream. His family surrounded him, but a part of him was caught in another world.

The door closed for the last time and Barbara poured them each a cup of coffee.

She brushed his shoulder with her fingertips when she placed his cup in front of him. She sat next to him. "Ed, it was just a dream. You act like someone died."

"Not yet. But I know they're going to. Every time I have a dream and have these feelings, it comes true."

He looked into Barbara's eyes. "You know it, too. You've watched my dreams come true with me. Before I started telling you about them, I thought that I was goin' crazy, that I was imaginin' them."

Ed looked down, and almost as if he were talking to himself, added, "But no one died before. Nothing bad was gonna happen. They were like an experiment, curiosity things. Not awful like last night."

He held his forehead in his hands. He sighed from the depth of his fears and shrunk into himself. "How can I sit here and not try to stop this? Still, I know that no one's gonna believe me. Except you. I know it! I don't blame them. I wouldn't believe me either, if I weren't livin' it."

Ed drew a deep breath and looked soulfully at Barbara. "You know what really scares me?"

He reached for her hand. "Your dad's going to California this weekend. What if it's his plane that's gonna crash? But if I tell him not to go because of last night's dream, he'll think I'm nuts. If I don't tell him and his plane crashes, I won't be able to live with myself."

A tearless sob escaped from Ed. "Barbara, what should I do?"

"Did you see Dad on that plane?" Barbara's eyes widened and she felt her chest tighten.

"No. I didn't recognize anyone."

Ed's face softened. "I'm sorry. I didn't mean to frighten you."

His face closed back up. "Not knowing anyone in the dream is one of the things that's confusing me. I've always known the people in my dreams. If each one of the come-true dreams hadn't affected me so physically, I wouldn't be so sure, but last night's dream left me with the same feeling. This dream's really spooking me."

Barbara put her other hand on Ed's. "Let's pray together. Maybe we'll know what to do then."

Ed opened their back door to let Barbara enter first. His shoulders drooped.

"Your dad thinks I'm crazy," Ed said.

"He thinks we're both crazy. You for having prophetic dreams. Me for believing you. We probably shouldn't have told him about the earlier dreams, how you had started telling me about them and how we'd both seen them come true. Did you notice how he seemed to back away from us without even moving his body?"

"Maybe I shouldn't have told him how I can feel it in my gut when one of those dreams happens. That was when he stood up and said that we were going off the deep end and to stop making him nervous about flying."

"His saying that he'll probably have a stroke from fear, thanks to us, has me scared. Ed, what if he did have one? We'd be responsible." Tears clung to Barbara's lower eyelids.

"I dread this weekend. If I go out to work on the control tower's radio, I'll want to listen for any hint of a crash."

Barbara cringed. "Let's not say anything to the rest of the family. No need to have them worrying, too."

She hesitated, and then added. "Unless Dad tells them. With his attitude today, I can imagine him making fun of us, ridiculing us. Oh, how I wish you hadn't had the dream."

"That makes two of us."

They both looked drained, exhausted.

Barbara and Ed watched the clock all day Saturday. Wherever they were, whatever they were doing, they mentally followed the progress of her father from Chicago to Los Angeles. There was no news report of a plane crash on the radio or the evening news on television.

That night, the exhausted couple lay in bed. Neither could sleep.

"At least Dad's safe," Barbara said.

"Yes, but he's probably telling your brother how crazy I am. Wait until MY brothers hear about this. They're gonna be saying, 'What can you expect from a man whose head was run over by a wagon when he was a boy?' This is gonna be hard to live down."

"I know. But you had to tell Dad."

"You're right. I couldn't have lived with myself if his plane had crashed. I guess we're not quite done worrying about him yet. He still has to come back home. At least, I'm pretty sure the dream plane was going toward the west."

"How can you be sure? You're talking about your dream as if it were a TV show."

"You're right about that, too. There isn't anything for sure. I'm glad there hasn't been a crash, but I keep expecting my dream to come true."

"Maybe it won't this time. There wasn't anyone you knew in it, like the other dreams."

"But I had the feeling. I'm afraid it'll happen. I wonder if I should've called the FAA."

"Do you believe that they would cancel flights because Ed Morse had a dream?"

"I guess not. Let's try to go to sleep."

Ed's father-in-law was back home for a week before a plane crashed in Colorado.

Ed searched for photographs of the wreckage in the newspapers, asking himself whether it was what he foresaw. None of the photos showed the terrain in the background. Nothing matched his dream...exactly.

He noticed that people looked at him strangely. He knew that his father-in-law had told his family and friends about the "good one" that Ed pulled on him. Some of them had teased him about it.

Then, after the crash, people stopped talking when he approached. He imagined the truncated conversation. "He thinks that he knew the plane was going to crash in Colorado. Who does he think he is?" He walked past them without blessing them with his familiar smile and warm handshake.

A sense of restless anxiety followed him to work and back home again. It hung around him like a fog becoming denser and denser until it insulated him from human interaction. Only Barbara could reach into it, but she was still an arm's length away.

Ed became bedridden by a strange malady. For an entire week, he wrapped himself in a cocoon of blankets. He poured all of his pain into Barbara's ear late into the night.

One morning, he realized that he'd used up the words for his aching fear. He arose for breakfast and began to pick up his old routines.

Ed still wondered why he had been given the dream, but he stopped feeling like he should have prevented the crash's occurrence.

In time, his engineering nature began to develop rational theories about it. He began to believe that the vision was the result of a series of coincidences. At the time of the dream, he had been maintaining and upgrading radio and electronic equipment in the control towers of small airports in central and southern Illinois and Indiana. Because this work was a moonlighting job on weekends, he was tired from working long hours seven days a week. Somehow, the physical exhaustion, coupled with the mental strain, broke down some sort of barrier so that part of him moved to another time and place.

The theory faded and Ed questioned whether he had foreseen the crash at all. He told himself that eventually, a plane was apt to crash in mountains somewhere, sometime. He was probably being presumptuous to think that he held a special message at a special time. Still he wondered.

Ten years after "the crash," as they called it, Ed and Barbara took their six children on a two-week camping trip, moving further west every three days until they reached Colorado.

"Your dad and I'd like to explore a little by ourselves," Barbara told their teenage sons Eddie and Francis. "Do you think you could keep this camp together and make the day fun for the younger ones?"

The teens looked at each other and grinned. "Sure, Mom," they said in unison.

Barbara showed them the food for lunch, where changes of clothes for the young ones were kept, made suggestions for the day's activities and gave them a list of prohibited activities and places.

"We'll be back by 5:00 p.m. Have fun," Ed called to their children from the rolled down driver's window.

Barbara looked at her two oldest sons and smiled, "Thank you."

She picked up the hand-drawn map that lay on the car seat between them.

"We're almost there. Another turn or two. I wonder if I'll recognize...That's it!" Ed pointed to the steep slope to their right.

His forehead wrinkled and his eyebrows lowered and squeezed his eyes. "No," he said under his breath and pulled the car off the road.

He stepped out of the car, shielding his eyes with his outstretched palm. "The lay of the land fooled me. I almost think I saw this road from that spot over there. It looks so much like my dream. But my mind must be playing tricks with me. The sweep of trees is missing. In my dream, that whole mountainside quivered with aspen trees." Ed helped Barbara see the spot he was talking about.

"Let's stretch our legs a little bit. We might as well enjoy the scenery," Barbara suggested.

"Okay." The wired tension slipped from Ed's shoulders but then tightened again imperceptibly. "After we walk, maybe we can drive on for a few more miles?"

An hour later, Ed swung the car around at a wide spot in the road. "I give up. Let's drive down off this mountain and have lunch."

"Are you sure you want to do that? We planned this trip so you could see the place for yourself."

"I know. But we aren't gonna find it with this map. Tell you what. The first little store or gas station we find, I'll ask for directions."

"Hello?" Ed called to the empty one-room store. His eyes adjusted to the cool artificial twilight made by the drawn shades. The shelves were lined with nonperishable groceries, hand tools, dusty boxes of nails, screws and bullets.

This looks like an unkempt museum display of goods from the last forty years instead of a business, Ed thought.

Barbara followed him inside. Her widened eyes scanned the room.

"Maybe we should have knocked on the door instead of walking right in. I feel like we're intruding," Barbara whispered in Ed's ear.

"I already called out. They might wonder if we high-tailed it out of here."

Barbara kept her hand on the doorknob.

They heard a scuffle at the back of the store. A white head peeped around the door. It was followed by the shoulders of a bent old man and accompanied by the sound of shuffling feet.

The man cleared his throat and croaked, "I thought I heard something out here. What can I do for you?"

Ed asked, "Do you have something cool to drink?"

"Sure. Pop or beer?"

"Two colas would be great. How much?" Ed asked reaching into his pocket, as the man toweled off the dripping bottles.

"Fifty cents."

Ed took coins from his upturned hand. "We've been driving around these mountain roads all morning. Beautiful country. I seem to remember that a plane crashed near here a few years ago."

"Sure did. If you came down that grade, you probably passed the place." The man's index finger pointed in the direction they had come from.

Ed's eyebrows squeezed together. "Past the crossroads?"

"Yeah. On the left a mile or so. I helped with the rescue. That's what they called it, but there weren't any survivors to save." The man looked at his feet.

"Sounds awful," Barbara empathized.

"Lady, I hope you never have to see anything like that. When I got there, they were taking a woman out of a seat and putting her in a bag. She haunts my dreams – not so often now. I was put to work searching the area for body parts. I won't go into that. I don't want to mess up your dreams, too."

Barbara and Ed's eyes turned from the man to each other at the same time, sending a silent knowing message to each other.

The man continued, "You'd think that bodies would be the part that was hardest to take. But, for me, it was a child's rattle shaped like a duck. I kept imagining the little hand that might have been holding it.

"I'm sorry. I don't know why I'm talking about this. I've told you more than you wanna know. My poor wife, bless her soul, had to listen to this over and over until I got it out of my system."

Again, Ed and Barbara shot each other knowing glances.

Ed took a sip of the cola. "We asked the question that started the memories. I'm sorry. I shouldn't have."

The man wiped his hands on the towel again. "Bless you. At first, my buddies and I talked about it. We each had our own horror. Would you believe that one of the guys was bothered by the fact that he found food, rice and that kind of stuff, in the tail piece? He kept thinking that those poor people probably smelled it and their mouths were watering in their last minutes. Funny, for most of us, our imaginations were harder on us than the reality of what we had to clean up."

A tear slipped down Barbara's cheek.

"Sorry, Lady. My wife used to say I got carried away about this wreck. I didn't mean to make you sad."

"It's all right. I cry in movies, too."

Ed leaned forward. "That place. I thought it had trees, aspen trees, in the background in the photographs. We didn't see any there today."

"You're right! They logged that mountain a year after the wreck. Took all the aspen out of the area."

Ed choked on his drink.

"Well, we got to get going. Thanks for everything." Ed sat his bottle on the counter.

"Hope telling us your memories doesn't leave it hanging over you."

"Have a good day," Barbara said, walking out of the door.

Ed and Barbara were unusually quiet on their way back to the campsite.

Ed relived the dream again and staged it in the place they had just visited.

Barbara recalled the nights of listening to Ed talk through the crash dream. She wondered if the wife of the man at the store had listened his way out of the accident clean-up, too.

When they drove up to the campsite, they saw their children sitting at the picnic table playing cards.

Jenny, the youngest, jumped up from the bench and hopped up and down clapping when she saw the car. She ran to open Barbara's door. "Mom, we had so much fun. Francis took me and Sue swimming. Eddie and the boys caught fish for our supper. I had a dream-come-true day!"

Barbara got out of the car and wrapped her arms around Jenny. She kissed the child on her forehead, nuzzled her fly-away curls and whispered in her ear, "It was a dream-come-true-day for me, too."

Uncle Eddie and his family stopped by our house to visit on a drive across the United States. We were finishing an impromptu meal that I had made for us.

Uncle Eddie noticed Raymond Moody's book *Life After Life* on our bookshelf. When he asked if Jim believed what was in the book, his family tensed up. When Jim told them about his out-of-body experience when he was exhausted from working in the potato fields, I tensed up, too.

Uncle Eddie told the story recounted above.

When I spent a weekend with Ed and Barbara a few years after Jim died, I heard it again. The story was the same but I heard more of the details that time. I had become more open to the idea that Eddie could see something different: he had stood in a different place than I had.

The Protectors

"Bob and I need to tell you what happened on our trip," said Ann in a hushed tone, looking around the library, as if making sure that no one overheard her request. "Can we go to your office?"

They acted with the urgency of characters in a spy novel but there was an underlying hint of giddiness. I was intrigued, because this was uncharacteristic behavior for this couple.

I liked spending time with Ann and Bob; it lifted my spirits to be with a couple who were so devoted to each other. As we walked to my office in the back of the health library, I thought about the times the three of us had researched the literature about Bob's condition. I had met them soon after Bob was diagnosed with metastatic melanoma. They were shocked at that time, but both of them were determined to learn everything they could about the condition and its treatments. Bob was an engineer and studied the medical books and periodicals systematically to understand the treatments offered and their efficacy. Ann was an educator in a large corporation and she concentrated on clinical trials and managing the common symptoms from Bob's treatments. When the melanoma recurred the second time, they decided to take a vacation before considering treatment options.

Walking back to my office, I considered the possibility that they had tried an alternative treatment while on their trip. It was reasonable for them to be concerned about telling me, an oncology nurse.

When we were settled in my office, Ann started to tell me about an incident that occurred during their trip. "We went to see my Aunt Ellen in Florida. She is into meditation and nutrition, those kinds of things. She has a lot of experience with healers and knows who's good, and who isn't. I asked her if she knew someone who could do a reading on Bob and she recommended a lady who reads auras."

Bob broke in, "I don't know how I let Ann talk me into it. The woman lived out in the middle of a swamp. The gravel road was bumpy and I kept expecting to see an alligator stretched out across the road."

Ann looked at Bob and laughed. "I really had to talk to get you to go. I think you agreed when I pointed out that you had tried all the regular cancer treatments and what could it hurt to give this a try."

Bob smiled into Ann's eyes and touched her arm. "I did it for you."

Almost apologetically, he looked at me and continued, "Wandering around the swamps of southern Florida looking for a woman named Sally who reads auras is not the kind of thing that engineers do. This is the 1990s, not the 1700s. I felt like I was going backwards hundreds of years."

Bob looked like an engineer. He wore blue jeans and a short-sleeved plaid shirt with a ballpoint pen in his right shirt pocket. His face showed the telltale signs of his forty-eight years, a few wrinkles around the eyes and a receding hairline. The furrowed forehead was more from worry about this situation and less from aging or the two years of cancer treatments.

Ann looked ten years younger than Bob. Her wrinkle-free face was framed in a pageboy, every strand of her dark brown hair falling naturally into place. She didn't need any makeup to enhance her large brown eyes and flawless skin. A sense of serenity emanated from her.

Bob and Ann continued telling me about the incident, seamlessly passing the story-telling baton back and forth. They pulled me into the scene.

The house with a porch across its front looked rather small in a clearing surrounded by ancient trees. It barely had any paint left on it. The gate hung askew on a rickety picket fence. There was no sidewalk, just a dirt path. And the wooden steps wobbled and creaked.

Bob worried to himself, This isn't the home of a successful healer.

When Ann knocked on the screen door, Bob tried to see into the house, but the front room was so dimly lit that all he could only see dark shadows. A short, stubby woman approached the door, calling out in a gravelly voice, "You Ellen's people?"

Ann called back, "Ellen's my aunt."

The woman opened the door, saying "Call me Sally." She led them into her sitting room and pointed to an old couch. She sat in a worn chair across from them.

Sally said, "Ellen asked me to see you, but she didn't tell me why."

Ann smiled at Sally and explained, "I have always admired Aunt Ellen's perceptiveness. She said that you are able to see things that most of us miss."

Ann explained, "Bob has cancer. We know that the mind can be a powerful force against disease. We need help because the doctors don't hold out much hope since it recurred."

Ann put her hand on Bob's pant leg, then she continued, "Bob feels good now, but we feel like we're stuck in limbo. Can you help us?"

Sally told them to just sit quietly for a minute, because she needed to settle herself.

When Sally asked them to put more space between themselves, to sit on either end of the couch, Bob became uncomfortable. He would have left but he knew that Ann wanted him to stay.

After they settled into their places, Sally took Bob's right hand in hers. Her hands looked small trying to reach around his big paw. Sally closed her eyes, but continued to hold his hand.

The quiet was broken by Sally's long sigh. She opened her eyes and looked directly into Bob's eyes. Bob felt like she was drilling into his soul.

Finally Sally spoke, "Bob, you're very ill, dangerously so. You're being protected by people who love you. That's what's keeping you going. They've all passed over, but they're here to help you. I want you to know who they are. Both your mother and your father are here."

Sally added, "There is an older man with gray hair, leaning on a cane that has a vine carved on it. Could that be your grandfather?"

"That sounds like Uncle Jerry. I never saw him without a cane like that."

Bob didn't tell Sally that he had his Uncle Jerry's cane now.

Sally described four more relatives, each holding or wearing something that made it easy for Bob to name them.

Bob was beginning to believe in Sally. He began to hope that his people really were nearby and protecting him.

Sally's forehead wrinkled and her lips tightened. "There's someone else who's about your age, Bob. Has one of your friends already died? The man is wearing a police uniform."

Bob denied knowing any one like that who had died.

Sally insisted on giving them more clues. She continued, "He has a mustache, dark hair and light blue eyes."

Bob shook his head.

Sally seemed frustrated that she couldn't find a distinctive feature like she had with the others. She said, "He has a mole on his cheek. He standing like a military man except for the odd way he's holding his right wrist with his left hand. Only three fingers are showing. His little finger is curled behind the wrist. Could the number three be significant? Or is it the way the three fingers look like an M or W?"

Bob blurted out, "You're describing my friend Will! But he's alive! I just talked to him a couple of weeks ago. I haven't seen him for five years. We used to get together and talk about old times every time I went back home. But since Mom and Dad died, I haven't been back there. Ann and I are going up to Pennsylvania to have dinner with Will and his wife Laura on Saturday."

Sally persisted, "The man's there. Even though we can't identify him, he's there because of you. That's what's important."

Sally took Bob's hands in hers and looked into Bob's eyes. "You're being protected. You have a golden aura around you and it's being held in place by these loved ones. Their light's guarding you against death right now.

"I can't read your future. I don't know if these people are doing this until your body gets well. Or, they could be there because you have some important work to complete. You're receiving a great gift and should use it well."

Sally squeezed Bob's hands one more time, and then let go of them. Bob thought the way Sally brushed her hands together, like she was whisking chalk dust off of them, was odd. Then Sally stood up and Bob knew that the reading was finished.

Sally and Ann talked about trivial stuff, but Bob was anxious to get out of the place.

54

When they got to the car, Bob asked Ann, "Can you drive? I'm exhausted."

On the way to Aunt Ellen's, Ann said, "I'm sorry about how this turned out. I guess that Aunt Ellen's recommendation wasn't that good, after all."

Bob began to laugh, "Sally sure had us going. I had been close to believing that Mom and Dad were there. But them putting an aura on me was too far out."

Ann agreed, "She got carried away with that man who looked like Will, too."

Bob wondered, "It was odd how I named everyone else. Do you think Sally has a batch of descriptions that she uses with everyone? Ones that are common and vague enough that people will match them to someone they know sooner or later. Anyway, once she described the person who looked like Will, I felt like we had been duped."

Ann added wistfully, "I wanted it to be true. To think of you being safe instead of this uncertainty."

Bob said, "This'll be a good story to tell Will and Laura when we get together the day after tomorrow."

Bob and Ann paused in their retelling of the incident and looked at each other. As if silently nudged by Ann, Bob continued:

We arrived at Will and Laura's an hour late. When I saw the dark house, I wondered if we should have phoned them that we were going to be late. On the other hand, an hour's delay is likely with a long drive like ours.

I worried to Ann, "Do you think they gave up on us? Or forgot about our dinner plans?"

We went up to the house and rang the doorbell. Finally, Laura answered the door. She wasn't dressed to go out and had a blank look on her face.

"I'm sorry we are so late," Bob apologized. "I guess you gave up on us. Anyway, where's Will?"

Laura's eyes clouded. She swallowed hard and choked out, "You didn't hear about Will?"

We both shook their heads.

Tears trickled down Laura's face and she whispered, "It's been ten days. He was killed in a freak traffic accident while on duty."

Laura invited Bob and Ann in and they talked about Will. Neither of them could bring themselves to tell her about the reading from Sally.

I was stunned by the story. It seemed like something from the popular television show *The Twilight Zone*. I was shedding the kind of tears that well up when I feel deep true emotions. I knew that Bob and Ann were sincere and credible witnesses.

They were both looking at me, as if waiting for my response.

"What an experience! So, how are you using your gift?" I asked.

Bob said, "I've begun by making sure that my daughters know how important they are to me and making sure that our relationship doesn't need any repairing."

Looking at Ann, he continued, "We're trying to decide how we want to live the rest of my life."

Bob and Ann gave me a great gift that day. They opened my mind to new possibilities. Since then, other credible witnesses have, in hushed, almost secretive tones, shared their extraordinary experiences with me. I am thankful for these expanded views of a safe, caring world.

An Unbearable Pain

"Can you make sure that I don't have pain?" Mary pleaded. "I don't think I mind dying, but I'm so afraid of pain. I hurt so much before my operation. I never imagined my stomach could grab me and hurt so much. I don't know if I could stand that again."

Mary was hunched over in a brocade armchair in her living room. She was wearing a bulky red robe, but it couldn't hide her thin frailty, evident in her gnarled fingers and gaunt face. Everything except Mary's piercing blue eyes seemed to be ebbing; she was at a low tide. All of her energy was concentrated in those two orbs. Their intensity was hard to look at for more than a second or two.

Hovering nearby, like an unobtrusive waiter in a fine restaurant, was Mary's husband Harold. Although he was standing still as a statue, I could feel his uneasiness. His fingers were clasped so tightly together that his knuckles were white. Yet, his arms hung loosely over his well-rounded abdomen. Harold was the picture of latent helpfulness, waiting for Mary to wind him up with detailed directions.

I thought, *I feel uncomfortable calling this elderly woman by her first name, but she told me to.* Nevertheless, I felt like I was spitting out a fur ball instead of saying her name.

"Mary, Harold's going to show me all your medications," I said. "We'll watch your pain very carefully. Your medication can easily be adjusted if it's not working."

I tried to reassure both Mary and Harold, "You don't have to wait for my next visit. Call me if you have any change in your pain or any other problem. Hospice also has a nurse available twenty-four hours a day, if you can't get me. We don't want you to suffer."

I closed the front door of their ranch style tract home near the sleepy downtown of a San Francisco suburb with a nagging discomfort. *What's bothering me? I thought. Is it because she is only the third hospice patient whose care I managed as a nurse volunteer? Is it her almost phobic fear of pain? Maybe, it's Harold. Can he take care of her without her directing his every move?*

Mary and Harold are a loving couple. They were both teachers, Mary taught English and Harold music. Harold's craftsmanship is easy to see. They both proudly pointed out the violins that Harold had made. Mary said that she enjoys poetry, especially when Harold reads it to her. Their only son lives in New York, so Harold's going to be Mary's only caregiver.

I played back the interview in my mind as I drove to my job at the health library. I reviewed her words, changes in her tone of voice, and her body language trying to find the reason for my uneasiness, trying to make sure that I wasn't missing a key fact.

Two days before the following week's appointment, Mary called. "I need help. I had that pain again. I can't stand it."

Her voice was distorted and hoarse. It had the tone of a frightened child calling out to its parents in the night after a bad dream.

"Mary, can you tell me about it?" I asked, trying to sound calm.

"Oh, it hurt so much. I couldn't move. It felt like my guts were twisting inside."

"Are you having the pain now?"

"No. But I'm afraid it'll come back and never go away," she moaned.

"How long did it last?"

"It seemed forever, but Harold said that it wasn't more than a half a minute."

"Mary, how often does it come? Every half hour? Every hour?"

"This was the first time."

"Do you think that you could wait until I get off work for me to come to see you?"

"I can do that."

"But, if you have that pain again, call me and we'll make a new plan. Okay?"

Mary didn't need to call me back before I visited her. There was no obvious change in her condition. We could only wait to see if the pain reoccurred.

It did.

At the next visit, we talked about the pain and medications.

"Mary, do you have any idea how much morphine it would take to mask one minute's spastic-type pain a week? It can be done, but with that high a dose, you would feel drowsy all the time and sleep a lot. Is that what you want?"

Mary replied, "I hadn't thought about that. I just was trying not to have that pain ever again."

Mary never did experience the long, physical pain she dreaded. Instead she had to live through a more unbearable kind of agony—one that neither of us anticipated. Medication was useless.

"Janie, can you come over now?" Harold said over the phone, punctuating the sentence with more of an exclamation point than a question mark.

Hearing his panic, I said, "I'm on my way. Can you tell me what has happened?"

"It's best if you come here. The door will be open. Just walk in."

Both Harold and Mary looked like crumpled rag dolls when I entered the living room. Mary was seated in her usual chair in the living room and Harold was on the sofa beside her. They looked stunned. They were just sitting there, holding hands, silent. I eyed Mary's posture, looking for signs of abdominal pain.

Neither Mary nor Harold looked up as I entered the room.

My mind had been spinning since Harold had called. This was the day their son Arthur was flying from New York with his wife and daughter.

Could Arthur have changed his mind? Was the flight delayed? Had Mary had a new kind of pain?

None of my musings fit the scene in front of me.

I asked, "Wasn't Arthur coming today?"

Up flew Mary's handkerchief covering her face. Her whole body sobbed, but no tears flowed.

Harold croaked, "He's dead."

I dropped myself onto the sofa beside Harold, speechless. We sat like three beings hit by a stun gun on a science fiction movie, breathing, but not moving, not talking. Just being.

Finally, words, or rather utterances, retched out of me. "How? What? When? Are you sure? No. Can't be."

How I hated not making any sense!

Mary spoke. "He had a massive heart attack. They were running for the plane. Arthur had the suitcase. He fell and then he died."

Mary collapsed on herself. Hands on her face, the tears finally flowed and flowed.

Oh, no! I thought. *Mary has always been afraid of pain. How could we have guessed it would be this kind of pain? This loss is so much worse than the cancer pain Mary feared. There are no medicines for this. To lose her beloved son, who was on the way to say good-bye.*

Could Mary have had a glimpse across the threshold that caused her fear of an unbearable pain near the end of her life?

Dream Girl

A hand shaking his shoulder wrenched Malcolm from his dreams. He struggled awake, rubbing his eyes open with the heels of his hands. A round face surrounded by wavy honey-colored hair bent over him.

"What?!" he croaked and pulled himself upright.

The young woman straightened herself and tiptoed to the foot of the bed. Her twinkling blue eyes locked onto his bleary brown ones.

"Good-bye," she said.

A wave of sadness gripped him.

The girl's solemnity lifted and the kind of smile that precedes a giggle crept onto her lips. She turned her back to him, looked over her shoulder one more time, waved a backwards good-bye and flitted from the room.

"Malcolm?" Polly turned towards him. "Something wrong?"

Malcolm was wide awake now. "Someone was in here. Did you see her?"

"You were dreaming. What time's it?"

He reached for the alarm clock. "Four o'clock. I'm sorry I woke you."

The apology was unnecessary; Polly was purring into sleep again.

Malcolm lay back down and pulled the covers around his shoulders. The dream left him unsettled. He checked the clock again and again.

Five, he thought. *Might as well get up. Silly of me to let a dream bother me. I'm a physicist—a rational person. This is a feeling, not a fact. Maybe if I slip into the kitchen and make a cup of tea, this nonsense will evaporate.*

Two hours later, the sunlight pried through the cracks in the shutters and rested on the book on the kitchen table. Malcolm held a nearly empty tea cup in his right hand. The tea-cozy lay next to the flowered teapot. Thoughts of the dream girl interrupted his reading once again.

Polly entered the room tying her robe around her waist.

"Morning, sweetheart." Polly's smile was more evident in the softening of her cornflower-blue eyes than on her lips. She leaned down and brushed a kiss on his forehead.

"You're up early," she said. "Would you like to have another cup of tea and some toast with me?"

Not waiting for his answer, she began making breakfast. "Looks like we'll have a nice Saturday. After breakfast, I'll make my grocery list, then call Elizabeth and see what she needs."

Malcolm interrupted, "Do you mind if I come along? The garden really doesn't need my attention today, but I would enjoy seeing Elizabeth."

"That's kind of you." Polly's eyes twinkled with delight. "She'd enjoy seeing both of us." Then, the light in her eyes ebbed and wrinkles pushed their way up her forehead. "You look tired, dear. Didn't you sleep well last night?"

"Remember me waking up with a dream? I don't understand why it's bothering me. Never did go back to sleep. It didn't feel like any dream I have ever had before. The hand on my shoulder was so real. It was the sort of shake our own little Alice used to give me after she had a bad dream as a teenager. Remember how she used to talk them away?"

He mused, "Such a sweet thing, this little dream girl. She didn't want to talk like Alice used to. All she said was, 'Goodbye.' She had pretty hair—the same color as yours was when we got married."

An hour later, Polly held her shopping list in her hand with a mossy green raincoat on her arm covering her purse. She placed her hand on the doorknob and hesitated.

Turning to Malcolm, she asked, "Do you mind if I call Elizabeth one more time? She must have been talking with neighbors when I called earlier."

Polly walked to the phone and dialed. The longer she waited, the more deeply her brow furrowed. "Still no answer."

"We could stop by before we shop, if you'd like."

"Let's do that, dear. This isn't like her. I'm beginning to worry."

"I hope she isn't sick." Polly stood in front of Elizabeth's apartment door, digging deep into her purse jingling and rattling metal objects.

"Did she say anything about not feeling well when you talked to her yesterday evening?"

"No. There they are!" Polly pulled a ring of keys from her purse, chose a silver one and put it in the lock.

"Elizabeth," Polly sing-songed into the opening door. "It's Polly. I have Malcolm with me."

Silence. No response.

They walked through the cramped sitting room, noted a grocery list on the kitchen table, and walked back to the bedroom.

They found Elizabeth still in her bed.

"She can't have slept through the phone call and our knocking on the door," Polly whispered, as another possibility crept in. Her eyes closed and she suppressed the arising "Oh-h-h. No-o-o," by clasping her hand over her mouth.

Malcolm stepped into the room, reached down and touched Elisabeth's gray hand. Cold.

"She must have died in her sleep." Malcolm waited for Polly's reaction; she was still standing in the doorway.

A moan squeezed past Polly's hand. "My sweet sister. O-o-oh. No-o.

She walked across the room, sat on the bed and clasped Elizabeth's hand one last time. "My dear sister. You were all alone. I'm sorry I wasn't with you. I miss you already."

Malcolm gently touched Polly's shoulder, tears streaming down his cheeks, too. He missed his kind sister-in-law already.

After the funeral, they had to begin the task of emptying Elizabeth's apartment. Each day, while Malcolm worked at King's College in London, Polly went to Elizabeth's apartment. Almost every day, Polly found another reminder of her sister's thoughtfulness.

"Malcolm, I want you to see what I found today. It's that tin on the table. Elizabeth intended it for our Alice."

Malcolm sat down and lifted the lid of the box.

"Read the letter on top."

He lifted the top paper and unfolded it. Polly stood behind him, looking over his shoulder.

They both read:

My Dear Alice,

I enjoyed the little notes and pictures you gave me. I like to look at them and remember you at the age you were when you made them. You are an adult now and will soon be having children of your own. I thought that they might enjoy seeing what you did when you were young.

At the bottom of the box, you will find a picture of me at the happiest time of my life.

Remember me.

Aunt Elizabeth

Tears dribbled down Polly's cheeks.

"That's just like Elizabeth." Malcolm refolded the note carefully.

Polly sat down beside him. "It's a shame she never had children of her own. She would have been such a loving mother."

One paper at a time, they reminisced about their child's bygone youth. They stacked the drawings and notes in the same meticulous sequence that Elizabeth had kept them.

When they reached the bottom of the box, Polly picked up the photograph and gazed at it tenderly.

"Wasn't Elizabeth a beautiful girl then? This was taken right before the war. Mummy and Daddy sent us to the country, like all the parents did when London was being bombed. We didn't know anyone there, you know. I didn't quite understand why we were sent away. Elizabeth watched out for me, made me brush my teeth and wash my face and hands before going to bed. Things like that. When I was pining away with homesickness, she made me eat—even found treats for me. You would have thought she was an adult the way she clucked around protecting me."

Polly sighed, "They cut her hair off at that place and she never grew it long again. What a shame. It was so beautiful."

Malcolm held out his hand and Polly gave him the photo.

He sucked in his breath. Then, he tipped his glasses to see the picture more clearly. "Do you remember when Elizabeth died?"

"Of course. How could I forget finding her in her own bed?"

"No. I was talking about the night before. I mean the early morning. When I was awakened by the hand on my shoulder and I thought it was a dream?"

Polly nodded.

Malcolm pointed at the photo. "It was Elizabeth. I didn't recognize her. She was an adult when we met. Is it possible that she was dying when she woke me?"

A sob ripped out of Polly's chest. She curled over and let the moan take her breath away. Then a storm of tears accompanied her sobs. She held her face in her hands.

"Why didn't she come to me? I would have <u>known</u> her. I might have understood. I'm the intuitive one; you're the scientist. We might have been able to save her."

Malcolm pulled Polly to her feet and held her close. His mouth was close to her ear. Softly, he said, "Maybe that's the point. Her heart was so bad that we had to do her grocery shopping for her. It left her so tired. I'm sorry I didn't recognize her. Do you think you would have seen her if I had awakened you?"

"I don't know. I do know that I miss her so much."

Almost six months after Elizabeth died; Polly told me the story you've just read. We were waiting for Malcolm to return to the hotel from work. For several summers, Malcolm consulted at Lawrence Livermore National Laboratory for a few weeks. When my husband Jim was alive, he worked with Malcolm. After he died, Malcolm and Polly invited me to join them for supper at least once during each of their summer stays.

Polly's retelling of the story was so heartfelt that I found myself crying with her.

"I still don't understand why Elizabeth woke Malcolm up and not me," Polly lamented.

I replied, "Have you thought that Elizabeth might not have been able to leave this earth if you had realized what was happening? She loved you so much. Bonds of love can hold people here a little longer."

Polly almost smiled, "I had never thought about that! Not saying good-bye because she loved me so much. Thank you. I see it differently. She may have been protecting me like during the war years."

Elizabeth had found a way to let her sister know that she was going to a good place.

RULES TO LIVE BY

Parents can only give good advice
or put them on the right paths,
But the final forming of a person's
character lies in their own hands.

Anne Frank

Dad's Three Guidelines

Dad didn't call them the "Rules for Success." That's what I named them.

He didn't even remember telling me about them. I know because I asked him. His response was, "Did I say that? Come to think of it, that sounds like good advice, but I don't know what makes you think it came from me."

Maybe he didn't say it like this: "You'll be successful if you're honest, work hard and accept responsibility."

But those are the guidelines that I thought came from Dad and have used since I was in high school.

I asked my brothers and sisters about "The Rules." They each had their own bits of wisdom that they attributed to Dad, but none of them were exactly same!

How did this happen?

I think that Dad's Rules for Success came from the examples of success that Dad held up for us.

Carl was one example. He only had a high school education, but he had risen through the ranks of the local rural electric company. He understood the practical applications of electricity and machinery and he worked well with people.

Dad, like many of the area's farmers, trusted Carl's advice. Carl was one of those "truth tellers," who delivered the results of his studies matter-of-factly, even when they didn't benefit his company or weren't convenient for his customers.

My dad admired the way Carl had climbed the company's ladder by his hard work. I think it tickled Dad that Carl supervised people with college degrees.

Dad told us, "Carl isn't afraid of work. When someone asks him to do a job, he doesn't point out that it's someone else's job. If it needs done, he'll do it."

From dinner table stories, like the one about Carl, I noticed that three traits were woven into almost all of Dad's character studies. I think that is how Dad gave me those Three Rules.

With each job I undertook, whether as a student, employee or volunteer, I tried to apply Dad's strategy for success. As a whole, the rules served me well. When I was younger, I thought that his advice would help me rise to the top—to be seen as a success.

An honest person gives a good day's work, whether or not anyone is watching. She can be trusted to use her time well and to handle machinery and goods with care, and to keep the system working, instead of working the system. Being honest means that there are no deals made behind closed doors. There is a consistency in an honest person's work.

Being honest also involves being truthful, not only to others, but also to oneself. An honest person is familiar with her strengths and weaknesses. She accepts herself as a work in progress and uses her strengths to compensate for the weaknesses. She doesn't need rationalizations or excuses. Instead she does the best she can do with what she has at the moment.

Working hard is almost an extension of being honest. A hard worker focuses on the job to be done. She values her accomplishments. Time clocks are devices to be tolerated, not the only way to measure the value of labor.

When my dad talked about accepting responsibility, he often described someone who didn't use a job description to avoid work. In any organization, there are tasks that don't quite fit into anybody's job description, but could be a part of anyone's work. Dad encouraged us to accept those with grace. He also taught me to make everyone's work easier by being cooperative.

Dad's Rules for Success provided me with a yardstick to measure my own worth.

Dario's Yardstick

Teachers need Dario's Yardstick. So do ministers, nurses, doctors, and anyone else in one of the "caring professions." Dario Cunial understood human nature and had pithy easy-to-remember sayings to live by. This yardstick helped Hedy and me put our situation in perspective.

My friend Hedy, who owned and managed our preschool Wee Care with me, had received a disturbing phone call the night before. Hedy told me the bad news while we were setting up the classrooms for the day at Wee Care. "Peter's mother called me yesterday evening. She's is taking Peter out of Wee Care. She also said that her two friends Mary and Sandy are taking their children out, too. Before you ask, she didn't say where they were going."

I couldn't hold back my greatest worry, "What if this is the beginning of a great exodus? It's the end of the month and maybe everyone's just waiting until tuition is due again."

Hedy and I had started Wee Care on a shoestring, promising our husbands that there would be paychecks for us. They both knew that we were discontented with the way the Park and Recreation District ran their preschool program. We wanted to do it "our way."

Three months before that mother's phone call, we had signed a year's lease on a wing of an elegant building which had been built as a rehabilitation center for wealthy alcoholics and had housed famous movie stars. We had opened our school in six weeks, even though more experienced people told us that it takes six months to get licensed. With the help of family and friends, we had converted the former suites into classrooms. We had painted and decorated the classrooms, equipped the facility and outdoor play area, passed city inspections, obtained a state license, and contacted potential families. Hedy and I had gambled, hoping that our reputations as preschool teachers would bring in enough children, and it looked like we were winning. Would our luck hold out?

Losing three children, and potentially more, could be disastrous. Yet, I don't think either the Wee Care students or their parents had a hint of our anxiety about Wee Care's future during classes that day.

That afternoon Hedy visited our friend Mary Ann who was still teaching for the Parks and Recreation District. Mary Ann wasn't home yet, but her husband Dario greeted Hedy. Dario was known for his commonsense advice and optimistic outlook. I think his attitude may have come from being the child of hard working, innovative immigrants from northern Italy or perhaps it was his years of teaching physical education at Horner Middle School, or maybe he was born with that wisdom.

Dario asked, "Why are you looking so glum, Hedy?"

"Some parents took their kids out of our school," Hedy replied.

"How bad is it? How many?"

"Three!" Tears welled in Hedy's eyes.

"How many students did you have?" Dario probed.

"Seventy."

Dario laughed. "What are you so upset about? Jesus Christ, the greatest teacher and communicator lost one out of twelve. When your numbers are as bad as his, come back and talk to me."

Hedy reported this conversation to me that evening. It didn't stop me from worrying, but it did relieve me of the awful feeling of not being good enough.

Dario's yardstick has served me well. I call it "The Jesus Christ Standard."

When someone complains about a teacher, a physician, or anyone who deals with people, I ask Dario's questions and apply his yardstick.

Three Wishes

It took two years for me to understand the advice that the middle-aged heart attack patients were giving me. I was a young nurse in my twenties working in an Intensive Care/Coronary Care Unit.

In the 1970s[3], the three days following a heart attack were critical. Fatal arrhythmias were most apt to occur during that time. So, the patients, who were usually men in the prime of their life, were placed on bedrest and wired to monitors that signaled their heart rhythms to us nurses and doctors. They also had at least one intravenous tube in their veins ready to receive life-saving doses of medications. We nurses not only watched for any changes in cardiac activity, we also did everything we could to reduce the load on their injured hearts. Men who had run companies, worked with heavy machinery, or jogged miles a few hours earlier were not even allowed to shave themselves. During this period of enforced rest when death seemed eminent, many of my patients reviewed their lives and expressed their regrets.

They told me what they wished they had done differently. The regrets varied and each person had his own unique set.

---

[3] Lifesaving angioplasty, stents, and coronary bypass surgery were not available.

Over time, I began to expect them to mention one or more of three regrets. They were:

→ I wish I hadn't spent so much time at work.

→ I wish I had a better relationship with my family.

→ I wish I had a better relationship with God.

Those Three Wishes reminded me of the importance of having balance in one's life.

I doubt if any of my patients would remember having given me these words of wisdom. I had listened to their reminiscing, like I had listened to Dad's role model stories, and found themes that could guide me.

Grandma's Sampler

I'M GLAD SOMEONE TOLD ME THAT

Wisdom is the reward you get
for a lifetime of listening
when you'd have preferred to talk.

Doug Larson

Be Careful What You Wish For

"May I tell you about the time I learned not to envy someone else's luck?" asked Ann.

Ann usually wanted me to help her find more information about her lung cancer treatments. That day she was asking for my attention.

I nodded towards two chairs in a corner of the library that offered privacy. Slowly, we walked over to them. I wondered if I'd get to see beyond Ann's carefully crafted appearance.

Ann's posture, clothing and impeccable grooming suggested her past dreams of stardom and hid her exact age. She dressed like a movie star from the early 1960s, wearing bright red lipstick and thick layers of coal-black mascara. Her black dress was tastefully, but boldly, accented with white and red. Not one black hair was out of place in the perfectly coiffed modified shoulder length page boy.

I thought, *How much time does it take for Ann to maintain this image? It must bother her that she can't cover up the raspy voice and occasional breathlessness from her cancer treatment.*

If I want to hear Ann's real story, I have to set aside my work and give her my full attention, I counseled myself. *Settle down. No thoughts about the report that's due. Listen with all your being and maybe you'll see the true Ann.*

As we walked, I felt my shoulders relax and my breathing slow down. I eased my concerns away until my world was reduced to Ann and me. We sat down facing each other. Ann leaned forward to touch my arm again and our surroundings receded further. It was like we had drawn a curtain around the two of us.

"Did I ever tell you that I was an actress?" she asked.

Before I could respond, she continued, "I was living down in LA then. I was trying to get into acting, while I worked as a waitress to support my three children."

"Remember the *Beverly Hillbillies*?" she asked, almost conspiratorially.

I nodded and she launched the following tale.

I was one of the girls in Jethro's dream sequence about being in a harem. I shared a dressing room with another girl in the harem. She had blonde hair. Her costume was lipstick red and mine was royal blue.

The director watched us come on the set and seemed pleased. When we were in our places, the director eyed the whole scene as if it were a painting. His eyes darted from person to person. Then, his gaze switched back and forth between the blonde and me.

He pointed to the other girl and me, "Your costumes aren't right. I want the blonde in the blue and the brunette in the red. Go back to Wardrobe and have them switch your costumes."

We were back in no time because they didn't have to make any alterations. We were exactly the same size!

The director's eyes lit up when we returned.

"Now that's right!" he said.

The other girl and I were in several more shows together.

One day, she was very excited when she came in to work; she had just signed a three-year contract with a studio.

That night, I went home wishing I was the one with the contract. It would have made such a difference for me. I could have supported my family on it and I would have been able to concentrate on acting.

I envied that woman. You know what envy means? That you want what someone else has. I wanted her contract. I wanted to trade places with her.

But, before her contract was up, I was glad <u>not</u> to be her.

Triumphantly, Ann paused, and then said, "You'll understand why when I tell you her name. The blonde woman was Sharon Tate."

Seeing the blank look on my face, she continued, "Doesn't that name ring a bell? Think back. It involved Charles Manson."

Was she the pregnant woman? I thought.

"You remember what happened to her now, don't you? Your eyes show it.

"When I first heard how they murdered poor pregnant Sharon, I thanked God that I was not in her place. After that, I never wanted to change places with anyone again."

"Ann," I said, "I'll never forget your story or your lesson. I admire your sense of timing and drama—just like a good actress."

Ann's smile spread across her face and rippled over her whole body. She looked around the room and sat a little straighter. With twinkling eyes, she tilted her head towards me. She drew a little closer and said, "I have lots more stories."

"I hope that I get to hear more of them," I said. "I'll bet they are as good as this one. Ann, you're a gifted storyteller. I wish that you would share those stories. Why don't you write them down for your children and grandchildren?" I urged.

"I'll think about it," she responded, eyes still sparkling.

"If you write them, I'll edit them for you," I countered, raising the stakes.

Ann replied, "Be careful what you ask for."

Less than a year later, Ann died. I hope that her family heard her stories. She didn't share any more of them with me. Having sampled this tidbit, I hungered for more.

When I'm wishing for something, I hear Ann saying, "Be careful what you wish for."

Nightmares

"I had that same old nursing nightmare again last night," Shiela said, her brow furrowing. She hesitated, and then continued. "It hasn't happened for a long time. I had begun to think that it had stopped haunting me now that I'm retired. I used to have it all the time when I was working." She looked around the room, adjusted her glasses and smiled slightly, as if asking for approval.

Five heads nodded, as if to say, "Go on."

Shiela took a deep breath, smiled tentatively and said, "Have you ever dreamed that you were at the end of your shift and realized that you had been assigned a patient that you had forgotten about? One that you had never even seen?"

Our heads nodded again, this time accompanied by sympathetic smiles.

"Last night, in my dream," Shiela continued, "I was having one of those days where I could hardly keep up with the workload, but my patients and I had survived it. I was sitting down to chart and looked up at the assignment board. I didn't want to believe what my eyes were seeing. There was another patient below my name! There had to be a mistake. Surely, not mine!"

The women laughed knowingly.

The laughter quieted and Shiela continued, "I sat there and felt an icy current run down my spine, and, at the same time, a burning sensation flashed from my toes to my scalp. A sweaty flush prickled the hairs on my head and upper body, but there was a shiver underneath. My hands gripped the chart and I examined the board again, wishing that patient onto someone else's assignment."

Shiela laughed. "That is when I woke up. I was having a hot flash. Boy, was I glad to be awake! Sometimes, the scene goes on and on, sinking into ridiculous horrors."

She looked around the room. "Have any of you had a dream like that?"

The friends' open smiles and sparkling eyes answered her question.

Eileen's cheeks reddened, almost to the color of her hair. "Yeah. But my nightmare usually involves forgetting to give medications. During the dream, I keep having the thought, *I can't believe that after all my years of nursing, I could do something so stupid. I wish this was a bad dream!*"

"I have that same *I wish this was a dream* thought that you do, Eileen," Liz said, in her throaty voice. Liz leaned forward with her hand on her chest, smiled broadly and exclaimed, "I have the dream that I have forgotten to give all of my patients their medications for the entire shift!"

"Now that I am retired, I'm free of that dream for months at a time," Karen said. "But the other night, I dreamed that I woke up late. I went ahead and got dressed in my uniform and went to work anyway."

As if preparing herself for work, Karen tugged at imaginary collar to straighten the points at either side of her neck. She continued, "I straightened my uniform on the elevator up to the floor. I went to 2 North and looked at the assignment board. Sure enough, my name wasn't on it."

Shiela interrupted, "Did you dream that you were going to work on your day off?"

"No," Karen responded with a wide grin. "Sharon was at the desk. She looked up and seemed surprised to see me in my uniform. She said, 'What are you doing here?' I just smiled at everyone there and said to them, 'I just wanted to see what it would feel like to get dressed and come back to work. I am so glad that I am retired.' Then, I turned around and went back home."

Laughter filled the room again.

"Does this mean that we have all had this nightmare of forgetting a patient or something else vital?" I asked, watching my friends' response.

The heads nodded affirmatively.

"Have you ever talked about this to anyone before?" Shiela asked.

This time the heads shook side to side.

"Someone should tell all the new nurses about it," Shiela said thoughtfully.

"I could write about it," I said. I thought, *This would make a good piece for my class. Lots of active voice. Several characters. It'll be easy to write.*

Back in my home office, I looked at the computer screen and was filled with disappointment. I thought, *Why can't I get past the first sentence? It seemed like such an interesting concept when we were sharing our common dream. Just look at this. Shiela's opening summary said it all. How can I use it to hook my readers? I can't believe that I'm stuck on the first sentence. The characters are flat and the topic isn't compelling.* I rewrote the first sentence over and over in my mind. Yet, none of the variations merited using the keyboard.

As I struggled with the words, I became aware of a familiar feeling. The nightmarish flush and shiver was creeping into me.

Could I be dreaming? I thought. Struggling to consciousness, I almost said aloud, *Thank goodness! Well, I do need to write something for this week.* Still not fully awake, I stayed in the scene, trying to rewrite the sentence. Gradually, the thought surfaced, *Oh, no! Your Nursing Nightmare has turned into a Writer's Nightmare!*

Integrity

Jim Concannon didn't tell me about Integrity; he told me about the most authentic man he had ever met.

Erik Erikson didn't tell me about Integrity; he wrote about it.

I studied Erik Erikson's theory of human development in nurses' training and it passed the "sibling test."

When I was studying Pediatrics, I assessed the theories and stages of child development by comparing them with my younger siblings. With brothers and sisters every two years, it was easy to mentally label each stage with a sibling's name. For instance, three-year-old development was "Mark" and two-year-old was "Mark last year." Since my siblings were smart, I dumbed down some of the developmental phases when studying.

Piaget's theories didn't make "sibling sense," but Erikson's did. I could see the first five of his eight cycles being played out in my siblings. Because of the validity in those stages, I accepted his final stage of Old Age with its struggle of Integrity vs. Despair.

Erikson wrote that, in Old Age, elders look back at their life. Those with Integrity are satisfied with the way their lives were lived. Those with Despair rail about missed opportunities and their conversations are marked by petty annoyances. His theory passed my "old people" test, too.

As a result, in my late teens, I set a goal of having Integrity by the time I was 80. I wasn't quite sure what it would look like, but I didn't want to become a complaining elder.

I didn't realize that I had an Integrity standard in my own life. It took Jim Concannon to point that out.

Dad became acquainted with Jim Concannon during the first year Jim and I lived in California. Dad wanted to meet some farmers. I was working the evening shift on the Intensive Care Unit at Eden Hospital in Castro Valley and hadn't met any farmers there. Jim, a student at Teller Tech, only met scientists.

Dad was not deterred. "Who's your priest? I'll go see him. He'll know some farmers."

Jim Concannon was one of the three contacts that Father Adams gave Dad. Dad visited them every time he came out to visit Jim and me.

One Christmas soon after Jim died, Dad asked a favor. "I'm going to put an extra package of smoked sausage in your Christmas package. Would you deliver it to Jim Concannon?"

When I gave Jim Concannon his gift, he told me, "Your Dad is one of the most authentic people I have ever met." It took me a year or two to understand that Authenticity and Integrity are almost the same.

Dad used to say, "I am who I am." He wasn't boasting or making excuses. He was simply being true to himself.

For example, when Mom was writing her memoir, Dad told us why he stopped going to school after the Eighth grade. "I figured I could make it without a high school education. Father Eggloff came out to talk to my Dad and told him that he should keep me in school. Dad agreed to send me to high school. When they told me that, I said, 'You can't make me stay. I want to be a farmer. I'm going to pick every good farmer's brain for all that I can. I'm going to get stuff together and farm.' And I did."

Dad wore bib overalls every day. They weren't only work clothes, they were who he was. When he dressed up for church, it was to please Mom.

At Lynda and Chris's wedding reception, Dad and his overalls gave me one of the best examples of what being true to yourself can do.

Lynda and Chris were married four months after Jim died and it was on Jim's birthday. Everyone expected the day to be bittersweet.

Lynda had told Dad that he could wear his overalls; Mom told him he couldn't. They compromised. Dad changed clothes after dinner before the dancing started. When Dad entered the room, there was a hush, like everyone inhaling at once, and then guys took off their ties and women shed their high heels. No one shed their dignity, but they became more genuine. Mom said Lynda's wedding was one of the happiest she had ever seen. Authenticity does that. It's contagious.

I'm glad that Erik Erikson explained human development in terms that I could understand. It led me to aim towards Integrity.

I'm glad Jim Concannon gave me that concrete example of Integrity.

Retirees' Regrets

A Chinese woman got my attention! She offered advice instead of expressing her regrets.

While working in a health library for ten years, I helped people find answers about their medical problems or treatments.

At least once a week, someone would say, "I didn't expect to spend my retirement dealing with this (name of medical condition). If I had known, I wouldn't have put so many things off until retirement." I didn't take the message too personally, but I did try to avoid habits that might lead to a chronic illness. Since I was still in my fifties, considering activities for my retirement was in a distant future.

One day, after I had helped a trim Chinese woman find medical information, she looked me in the eye and ruefully offered this advice, "Don't put off doing the things you want to do until the future, like I did. If you want to do something, do it now while your body is young and healthy."

That's how my five-year-plan arose. For two years, I prepared the groundwork for a three-year sabbatical. I taught other people how to do my job and slowly divested myself of responsibilities. Volunteer activities were wound down. Finances rearranged.

The three years of retirement/sabbatical passed quickly. I spent time with my grandchildren. I traveled, played, socialized with old friends and family, made new friends, gardened and learned more about writing and living.

At the end of that time, I was ready to rejoin the workforce, expecting not to have the typical retiree regret.

Importance of a Good Job

I don't want to end up like him, thought Mark glancing at the bald-headed man seated at the table. Something about the man unsettled Mark.

He was relieved to feel himself slip into familiar testosterone-rich territory when a smiling Barbie-esque teen walked through the door. A wide smile leapt onto his lips and his blue eyes flashed. He pulled his head back like a fisherman pulling in a big catch. She moved toward his station behind the cash register.

"May I take your order?" he asked.

Mark enjoyed working at McDonald's. He had started the job when he turned sixteen. Now he was one of the "old employees" and had helped train most of the current staff. The manager was a good guy and readjusted Mark's schedule each quarter to fit his classes. The job gave him enough money to pay for gas, Friday night ballgames, and dating. It was a good job for someone in school, but he intended to get a "real job" as soon as he got out of school.

The troublesome feeling resurfaced. *Why would an old man like that guy over there want to work here?*

As he took customers' orders and money, Mark peeked at the man talking to his manager. He observed that the old man wasn't nervous like most people applying for a job. He smiled every once in a while.

It looks like he's interviewing the manager! Mark thought. *They're standing up. Smiling at each other. Shaking hands. Oh-oh. They're coming over here.*

"Mark, I'd like you to meet our new employee, George Rains," the manager said. "He's going to start here next Wednesday on the early morning shift. He'll be taking care of the dining area."

"Glad to meet you," Mark pasted on a smile and stiffly reached across the counter with his right hand extended, while thinking, *I can't believe Mike is hiring this old codger. The old guy must be are real loser, probably can't get a decent job.*

Turning towards the manager, Mark inquired, "Will I be showing him the ropes, Mike?"

"Why, yes. You do that well. I'll take him downstairs to get his uniform and I'll go over the usual stuff with him. Keeping the front dining area tidy isn't very complicated. Mostly, I need you to remind him where to check in, that sort of thing."

When they were out of sight, Mark puzzled, *Is that Mike's way of telling the old guy that anyone can pick up trays and trash left by lazy people?* A judgmental uneasy feeling tugged at Mark.

That evening, the aroma of fresh baked bread and the sizzle of frying meat greeted Mark when he opened the back door.

He sniffed the air and grinned.

"Mom, that sure smells good." Mark gave his mother a quick peck on the cheek.

"How was work?" she said without looking up. She asked both Mark and his father this every day.

"Same," he replied. "Can I slice the bread for you?"

"Thanks. Cut seven slices. You're wanting to eat one right now, aren't you?"

"Mom, you're treating me like a little kid, darn it. How did you know I couldn't wait for supper?"

The toasty heat from the bread warmed Mark's hand. He tapped the loaf with the knife handle. He smiled at the hollow drumlike sound. When the knife's blade bit into the bread, a waft of yeasty steam was released.

"This is perfect! McDonald's can't compete with your kitchen." Mark stacked the freshly sliced bread on a small plate, reserving one piece for himself.

He opened the refrigerator. He pulled the butter out and asked, "Have you ever heard of a man named George Rains?"

"No. Why?"

"Just wondered. He's starting work at McDonald's. He's awfully old for our place. McDonalds is for first jobs, not for old people."

Within a month, the morning customers at McDonald's knew that George worked on Mondays, Wednesdays and Fridays and wished he was there on the other days to greet them. George called them by name. Some of them began to drink their coffee "in house" on George's days, instead of hurrying out to their cars with their styrofoam cups in hand. For those, George set the table with the appropriate utensils, napkins and coffee additives.

Mark noticed how the days that George worked went faster. He didn't feel tired at the end of the shift. Customers were more cheerful.

Another month went by and Mark noted that people were coming to McDonald's and staying to visit with one another on George's days. They were arriving in groups. The McDonald's staff began to call these groups "George's coffee clubs." George knew the clubs' patterns and always had the furniture arranged with the right number of seats for each group. Some groups helped George rearrange the furniture to accommodate the following club.

Soon George's people started calling Mark and the rest of the staff by name. They began to ask Mark how school was going or what classes he was taking while they waited for their food.

On Mark's birthday, George's people wished him, "Happy birthday!" He knew that George had told them.

That night Mark's family celebrated his birthday, too. When his mother was cutting his cake, Mark said, "Would you believe that customers were wishing me happy birthday at work today? That George is too much. How does he know so much about people?"

With a twinge of sadness, he added, "I'm going to miss him when I graduate and get a real job."

George wasn't at work when Mark arrived the following Wednesday.

"It's Wednesday today, isn't it?" Mark asked the other cash register attendant.

"Sure is," Lois responded, and then added, "Wonder where George is?"

Mark looked at his wristwatch again, his brow furrowed. "He's always here on time. He's usually early. Hope nothing has happened to him."

Mark looked at the clock frequently. Sometimes the minute hand hadn't made a complete circuit of the clock's face.

"Fifteen minutes late! I'm worried," Mark said.

"Why don't you call George's house?" Lois suggested.

Almost as an afterthought, she added, "Maybe he's having car problems."

A smile almost crept onto Mark's face when he thought about Lois's car. *Funny that she would mention car trouble. She must worry about getting to work every day with her rolling, rumbling hunk of junk. I'll have to remember that if she's ever late.*

Mark nodded. "Good idea. It's slow now. I'll call him before anyone else comes in."

Mark decisively walked toward the pay phone, fingering the change in his pocket. He opened the phone directory and found George's name. He dropped the coin in the slot. Consulting the directory one more time, he dialed George's number. It rang, and rang, and rang. He hung up defeated. Concern pulled his hairline down and his eyebrows together.

"No answer," he said, returning to his post.

George's first Wednesday group began to trickle in. Each one noticed George's absence and asked, "Where's George?"

Mark or Lois replied, "Don't know." Or, "He's not here yet." Or, "No one's answering his phone."

Instead of a steady flow of muted laughter, Mark heard dark mumbling and saw heads shaking. One of them, Fred, rose up from their midst.

"I'm going over to George's house and get to the bottom of this," he announced.

"You do that," one of the group said. "We'll wait here for you."

Before Fred returned, John, one of the guys from George's next coffee club, arrived. He removed his cap as he entered the door. His head swiveled towards the people seated in his club's place and, for a moment, he looked disoriented. His eyes searched the room. He hesitated, and then approached the counter.

"Where's George?" John asked.

Before Mark could respond, Wanda called out from the first group, "George isn't here. Fred has gone over to his place to see what's wrong."

The groups merged and worried together.

When Fred's little blue sedan pulled into the parking lot, Wanda called out, "Fred's back. He's alone."

Everyone watched Fred park, open his car door and unfold himself.

"It's not good news," Wanda said. "Look at Fred's face."

Twenty sets of eyes studied Fred's features as he approached the door. Twenty legs resisted the urge to meet Fred and get the news sooner. He barely stepped inside the door.

"George," Fred started. His voice cracked and his eyes watered up. He swallowed, and then cleared his throat. "He's had a heart attack."

The room moaned.

Fred looked over their heads. He seemed to talk to the walls. "I rang the doorbell. No one answered. I knocked on the door, too. Bertha's his next door neighbor. She came out and told me that they took George to the hospital in an ambulance. Bertha's husband Leo drove George's wife Helen to the hospital. Leo told her that the Emergency Room doctor told Helen that George had had a heart attack. They put him in Intensive Care."

Heads were shaking; mouths were down-turned. Tears trickled down some of their cheeks. The room was silent.

Wanda looked around at the sad faces and suggested, "Let's take up a collection to buy him some flowers. I'll go to the florist and get a nice arrangement for George."

Mark had a thin brown paper sack in his hand when he opened the back door of his home.

He was relieved to find his mother in the kitchen. She listened sympathetically as he told her about George.

Finally, he pointed to the bag he had placed on the table between them and asked, "Do you think it would be okay if I took a card to work for people to sign it for George?"

His mother took the card out of the bag, looked at the front. She opened it and saw that Mark had already signed it with, "Get well quick. Mark."

"Good idea," she said putting the card back in the bag. "That'd do George a world of good."

The next evening Mark had another brown bag in his hand when he entered the kitchen. He didn't wait for his mother to acknowledge his presence.

"Mom, you'll never believe how many people asked about George! And it wasn't even his workday. I don't know how they all knew about his heart attack. All I could tell them was that George was in the hospital."

Mark's mother nodded her head and walked to the refrigerator with a glass in her hand.

Mark continued, "You should have seen their faces when I pulled the card out and asked if they wanted to sign it. Sometimes they would take it to a table and pass it on to someone else.

"By the time I left work the card was full."

Mark's mother filled the glass with milk and handed it to Mark. "Did you mail it? I didn't notice you getting a stamp for it this morning."

Mark looked at the table and shrugged his shoulders. "I took it to the hospital. The volunteer in the lobby told me that she would deliver it to George."

Anticipating a surprised look from his mother, Mark added, "Then I bought another card. I figure George's Friday clubs would get upset if they found out about today's card."

Mark's mother smiled, but didn't give him the pat on his hand, like she wanted to. "I think that is a smart move," she said, avoiding the word "sensitive" that came to her mind.

"Hey, Mom," Mark called out Friday evening. "Where are you?"

"In the family room," she replied.

Mark followed the voice, wearing a grin.

"I see you are carrying another card for George."

"Yup," Mark replied, holding up a white bag. "Got this one at the hospital gift shop when I took today's card to George. I got to deliver it myself. He had had heart bypass surgery. It was kind of scary going to his room. I thought he would be hooked up to all kinds of machinery. His nurse said he was doing very well and got off the ventilator really fast. He looked more normal than I expected. I mean not scary.

"His nurse asked if I was his son. Before I could tell her I worked with George, he said, 'I would be proud if he were my son.' Imagine that!"

Holding up the bag again, Mark said, "I got two cards this time. Lots of people asked about George today. Some of them asked if they could sign the card for him, even before I offered. Seems like these old folks have their own telegraph system! I figured I would take one into work tomorrow and leave one with Lois. She's working Sunday."

Mark's mother smiled and looked at Mark with a tear caught in either eye. "Those cards are good medicine for George."

Then, she added, "I think George may have rubbed off on you."

Signing cards with words of encouragement became a routine activity at McDonald's. Mark delivered them to George every day. When he couldn't make the delivery, he arranged for one of his co-workers to do it. George welcomed them into his hospital room, then his home.

One day it dawned on Mark, *George is greeting us, just like he did people at McDonald's! Instead of getting us napkins, he has been making sure he has soft drinks, coffee, cake or cookies for us. It seemed so natural, I didn't notice it.*

Mike the manager squeezed Mark's shoulder. "Did you hear that George is coming back to work next Wednesday?"

Mark handed change to the customer in front of him and turned to look at Mike. He wasn't smiling as Mike expected. Concern was written on his face.

"Yeah. Have you arranged for some extra staff for that day?" Mark asked.

A sense of dread dampened Mike's enthusiasm. "Are you saying George isn't well enough to handle his job?"

Mark smiled broadly and waved his right hand. "No! That's not it. I'm worried about all those people coming in to see George. It's going to be a zoo! I wish George worked during the dead time in the afternoon. It'd be so much easier."

Mike nodded as Mark spoke.

With a hint of a smile, Mike said, "I've got an idea! Let's give George some of his own medicine during that slow time of the day."

Mark thought he knew Mike's idea. "You mean, have a party here for George?"

"Sure do. I'm going to call George right now."

That is why the marquee in front of McDonald's read:
GEORGE RAINS IS BACK
FREE CAKE AND COFFEE
WITH GEORGE 2-3 PM 10/19.

I saw a sign like this at McDonald's when I was visiting Mom and Dad in Indiana. George was my uncle and there was a welcome back party for him. My mother told me the party was because Uncle George meant so much so many people. Groups came for breakfast because George was there and he made them feel comfortable and welcome. The management was celebrating Uncle George's return to work. At the time, I was surprised that someone doing such a humble job could make such a difference.

Uncle George taught me that any job can make a difference in people's lives. No job is small if it is performed with dignity.

The rest of the story is fiction. I wrote it to help myself understand Uncle George's impact on the people around him. I feel sure he would have behaved the way I described.

FULL CIRCLE

Once you learn how to die,
you learn how to live.

Morrie Schwartz

A Lesson from My Gardenia

I asked my sister Lisa, who is a landscaping and gardening expert, to look at my gardenia when she visited in the summer of 1996. I was worried and confused by its appearance. Each day a few leaves dropped off and the remaining leaves were slowly turning yellow. On the other hand, the air around the plant was perfumed by the gardenia's prolific blooms.

I was prepared to give the plant any fertilizer or soil amendment that Lisa might suggest. If she found that it was infected with a garden pest, I'd spray it as needed. But, I was not prepared for her blunt advice.

"This plant is dying," Lisa said. "You might as well go down to the nursery and buy a replacement."

"But," I retorted, "it has so many blossoms. How can it be dying?"

Lisa explained, "Plants under stress, like this one, make one last vigorous effort to bloom. They are trying to produce seeds — to leave their legacy."

Despite my sister's advice, I left the plant in the ground, hoping to nurse it back to health by the next spring. But, when my husband Jim and I came back from a month-long vacation, the gardenia was all brown. It had died, as Lisa had predicted.

I stored her wisdom away, wondering if I could ever apply it to anything in my life. I'm surprised that I didn't immediately appreciate the significance of the gardenia in my own life.

Only a few months earlier, on May 8th, Jim had been diagnosed with lung cancer. Three months after Lisa's visit, on October 21st, he died. In between those dates, we had an incredible number of blossoms in our lives. When Jim had the energy, we visited with friends, continued to explore our world and tried to build memories with our children. During that time, our whole community blessed us with loving attention. Greeting cards and prayers poured in from all over the world. Friends and family cooked Jim special treats and included us in their family celebrations. We were surrounded by love and good will. Jim's gentle nature flourished in that atmosphere.

Likewise, at hospice, I have marveled at this final blossoming that can occur when a life is coming to an end. Too often people think that hospice's work is only about pain control and helping the family care for the patient. The real work of hospice is providing the support to terminally ill people and their families so that they have a chance to burst forth in bloom, even as they die. Just like my gardenia, Jim and Hope Hospice's patients try to bring their lives "full circle." For Jim, it was critical that our children know how much he loved them and he took many opportunities to reinforce that. Each person has their own last legacy that they want to leave behind.

As a hospice volunteer, I was privileged to witness this time and again. For instance, one morning, as I walked into the room where my patient, a young mother was cradled in her parents' recliner, I was more deeply affected by the sight before me than by a masterwork in a great museum. Her teenage daughter was sitting on the floor with her head on her mother's knee. They were both bathed in a ray of golden sunlight that matched the angle of the mother's arm extending to her daughter's head and her daughter's strawberry blonde hair sparkled in the sunlight and her mother's love.

Each person has their own legacy that they want to leave behind. I hope that when I die, my loved ones will be nearby and the hospice philosophy will be evident in my care. I expect to be escorted into the next life by Jim, Mom and Dad, Grandma Holscher, Joyce, Bernie, Jean, Dot, Wendy..... In the meantime, memories of them bless my life. I have learned from them to live fully, blossom prolifically and appreciate miracles.

Lessons Learned?

"Can you choose the time you die?" I asked myself when Charles's daughter finished telling me about his death.

At the end of her tragic story, I told her, "What a gift you girls gave your father! How many parents get to see the lessons they've tried to teach their children actually lived out in the last moments of their life?"

I had known "The Six CCs" for more than a decade. Charles Conti was the only male CC. He and his wife Celeste named their daughters Carol, Christa, Connie, Charlene, and Cathie. The family thrived on lively discussions bordering on dissention, but united their CC shields against the outside world to protect each other. The girls looked alike with their dark hair and large brown eyes, but their personalities were distinctly different.

The girls had all started their own families by the time Charles was diagnosed with Parkinson's disease. They all admired how their father adapted to each new restriction the ever-progressive disease imposed on him. Over time, they had each participated in his research of schemes to rise above each new limitation.

When Charles was diagnosed with colon cancer and needed surgery, there wasn't time for his methodical studying. Worries about the effect of the Parkinsonism were brushed aside by his medical team. The ensuing aspiration pneumonia and steady decline eroded the CCs' confidence in the medical team. The girls spun off in different directions trying to find a way to bring their father back to health. Carol prayed, Christa threatened law suits, Connie researched medical literature, Charlene filled his room with family pictures, and Cathie questioned every nurse about every procedure and medication. Celeste stayed at Charles's bed side day and night. Still, Charles's health deteriorated. He was moved to the Intensive Care Unit where nurses only opened the door for family members.

The girls took turns staying with Charles and Celeste, but one morning they all felt an urge to visit him before going to their jobs. All of the CCs were in Charles's tiny room. His nurse came in to perform a procedure on Charles, so the others decided to have breakfast in the hospital cafeteria.

As they walked through the big double doors, a social worker called after Celeste, "Could I talk to you for a minute?"

Celeste said, "Girls, go ahead. I'll be with you in a few minutes."

The girls talked about what they could do for their father.

Connie said, "Maybe it's time we also think about how to help Mom."

Carol agreed, "Whatever she wants to do next, I'll support her."

"Yes. We'll take care of Mom," Charlene said.

"So, we're in agreement?" Connie asked, looking at each of her sisters in turn. As they nodded their heads, the pager announced, "Code Blue - ICU."

"That's Dad," one of them said. They leapt from their seats and ran. They ran up the stairs and to the nurse-controlled door.

"How are we getting in?"

"I can do it," Connie said, punching some buttons on the controller.

They ran to Charles's room. A team of doctors and nurses surrounded Charles' bed. They were counting off as someone pushed on his chest. His face was almost covered by the mask attached to a bag which was being squeezed periodically. Someone else was drawing up medicine in a syringe. Another person was poised over him with a curving clear tube. Their mother stood at the foot of the bed looking stunned. The social worker was at her side. They heard the social worker ask their mother, "Do you want them to continue the code? To intubate him?"

The girls circled around Celeste. Charlene touched Celeste shoulders from behind and spoke into Celeste's ear, "Mom, whatever you decide, we agree to it. No discussions. You decide."

Celeste looked from Charles to each of her daughters.

"Should we stop?" she asked.

"If that is your decision, it's the right one," Carol said.

"Stop," Celeste said, "Let him be. He's gone."

The daughters and mother hugged; the medical team began to pack the equipment.

"Wait," Connie said. "You can't go."

"I thought we agreed," Carol said.

"Not that," Connie said. "We all have to pray for Dad."

The medical team continued packing equipment.

"You, too," Connie said looking at the doctor.

"I have patients to see," he said.

"My dad's your patient. You can't walk out. My dad prayed every day of his life. Even when he could barely walk, he struggled to the front row at church."

Connie commanded, "All of you join hands with us. We're going to pray, like our father did."

Hesitantly, the group formed a halo around Charles' bed.

Celeste started, "Our Father..." and they all joined her.

If you could have looked into Charles' room at that moment, you would have seen the CCs circling Charles and holding hands with the medical professionals.

Charles's life finished as he had lived it—surrounded by his family and in prayer. What an amazing thing to happen in an ICU room!

Did Charles know the girls had all agreed to take care of Celeste when he stopped breathing?

WHY

Nothing is a waste of time
if you use the experience wisely.

Auguste Rodin

Make a Will

Anyone who knows the story of my cousins Merle and Randy Halter would recognize the importance of having a will.

Aunt Loretta and Uncle John were in their 30s when they died. Their boat was swamped in a rain-swollen ditch south of Vincennes. Their 8-year-old son Randy, who was wearing a life jacket, was pulled ashore by a friend who was also in the boat. Surely, Randy witnessed his parents drowning.

Eleven-year-old Merle was in another boat with two other friends of his parents. They were around the bend of the river when he heard his mother cry out, but believed that his dad was teasing her with a lizard or some other wild creature.

That tragedy on Mother's Day left a scar on many hearts.

Even before the funeral, families began to worry about where Merle and Randy would go. I heard Mom and Dad talk about taking them in, "Merle is Henry's age. Randy is just a little older than Jim."

"Will the boys' bedroom hold two more?"

"The girls' room has four."

"We can't take the place of John and Loretta."

"They would be two more mouths to feed."

"Two more kids at once will be hard."

"They'll have summer vacation soon and we can work it out."

Other families must have been having similar conversations. I don't know where Merle and Randy stayed while the funeral was planned.

Uncle John was Mom's cousin and had grown up on the farm uphill from her family home. Aunt Loretta was Dad's sister.

Both the Halters, who were Uncle John's family, and the Holschers, Aunt Loretta's family, wanted the boys. All they could agree on was that the boys shouldn't be split up. My Grandpa Holscher talked the authorities into letting the Holschers take care of the boys.

Merle and Randy went to live with Dad's sister Aunt Emma and her husband Uncle Ray. They didn't have any children. Ultimately, as my mother kindly said, "It didn't work out."

The boys still stayed with the Holschers though. Aunt Ruth took them in. Aunt Ruth had been widowed two years before the accident. She and Uncle Meinard had three children who were teenagers.

The worst day of Merle and Randy's life was made worse because Aunt Loretta and Uncle John didn't have a will stating who they wanted to take care of their sons.

That's why Jim and I made a will, even though we didn't have any property or financial assets. We had a more precious asset, our children. If something should happen to us, we wanted them to be in a secure and loving home.

Seatbelt On?

"Does everyone have their seatbelt on?" I always ask before driving away.

If anyone objects, I tell them about the accident that Lisa witnessed and they "buckle up."

Lisa was sixteen years old. She was an inexperienced, but careful driver.

The day of the accident, she came home in tears, "The car in front of me was hit and I didn't know what I should do."

The accident happened in downtown Livermore at P and Second Streets. A Volkswagen Beetle was hit on the driver's side by a car that didn't stop at the stop sign. Neither car was going fast.

Lisa told me that the driver was thrown out onto the sidewalk through the passenger door.

I called the police and gave them our contact information. I told the officer how upset Lisa was and asked that someone call us and tell us how the woman was doing.

In the meantime, I comforted Lisa telling her that the worst I could imagine was that the woman might have a broken leg or pelvis.

When the officer phoned an hour later, he said, "I'm sorry to tell you that the woman died at the scene. She had a head injury."

He asked, "Your daughter is still in high school, isn't she?"

"Yes," I replied.

"The good news is that the driver of the car behind her is a credible witness. Your daughter won't be needed as a witness."

When we read the newspaper, we learned that the woman wasn't wearing her seat belt. Her two children were in the back seat. They were wearing seat belts and weren't injured, but they did witness their mother's death.

The tragedy didn't end there. The woman's husband was depressed after his wife's death and had a hard time managing his family alone. About two years after the accident, the father committed suicide with a gun. His son found him.

Our family has always thought that these tragedies could have been avoided if the woman had worn her seat belt.

That's why everyone in my car has their seat belts buckled before the car moves.

Corking Vesuvius

It's gone, but I guess I don't need it anymore, I thought, surprised at the lingering confusion. The forty days of Lent had passed without me using it once during that time. *Why am I not excited about being free to indulge it again?* I worried. I didn't realize it then, but at the age of twelve I had just conducted my first life-altering self-improvement project.

That year, Lent arrived and I was bored with the idea of giving up candy, or doughnuts, or another food, like my friends and I had done since the first grade. Instead, I wanted to test the limits of my will-power, to give up something that seemed impossible to do without. That is how I stumbled on the idea of trying not to "lose my temper" for the entire forty days.

Putting a cork in my Vesuvius was not easy. I was the oldest child in our family and had found that spewing my white-hot anger resulted in others deferring to me. Although hitting and kicking was not my style, I could resort to them, if needed. My preferred weapon was words. I could hurl barbed insults, expose weaknesses, stab the underbelly of shame, and deploy blasts of heated self-importance quite effectively. My younger siblings usually bore the brunt of my roiling anger. Yet, away from home, my shyness hid the volcanic aspect of my nature.

For forty days, I reasoned instead of erupting, I would think, *Do I really want that? How can I get them to do what I want without losing my temper?* At the same time, I worried, *They're going to think I'm weak and never do what I tell them to do again.* I had to reassure myself that they would fall back in line once Easter came and I could unsheathe my anger once again.

About two weeks into the experiment, I started to notice something changing. By using the *voice of reason*, instead of the *voice of anger*, I was getting more cooperation and I liked myself better. I found that clearly and gently stating my case encouraged an even-handed discussion. With this approach, I could stand firmly on my position and didn't need to attack or defend myself. I discovered that listening was a stronger tool than red-hot words.

Lent ended. Listening was replacing sharp words.

Behind Closed Eyes

When our children were young, they weren't sure whether their dad was working on an idea or not. Even after he came home from work in the evening, he continued to mull over equations and think about the problem he'd worked on that day. He often did that thinking in his easy chair with his eyes closed and his feet up. Theoretical physicists like to think and Jim often said, "I can think better with my eyes closed. It reduces distractions."

We were not the only ones confused by Jim's special way of working.

One time, our friend Harlan wanted to replace the pipe running from the street to his house. He was an electrician and he asked two of his "construction" friends and Jim to help him one Saturday in the early summer.

All morning long, they dug and dug. By noon, the trench was six feet long and they had another twenty feet to go. The sun was hot, and the men were all sweaty and hungry. Jim was tired, too.

After lunch, Jim did not pick up his shovel and dig with the other men. He said, "I need to have another Fresca and I want to think about this job."

Harlan wanted to say, "Jim, you're embarrassing me in front of my friends. Why don't you dig, like the rest of us?" He worried that his friends Paul and Harold would make fun of Jim, talking about how lazy he was sitting in the shade and say that he wasn't a "real man." Harlan thought, *Maybe Jim isn't like us, after all. He always seemed like a regular guy. Now, I'm not so sure.*

Jim didn't go to the backyard to think. He didn't go into the house. He sat right beside the house and watched the other men work while he thought about getting the pipe out of the ground!

Jim finished his soft drink and thought some more. Finally, after a whole hour of thinking, he stood up and walked to the trench.

"I've been thinking. There should be an easier way to do this."

Harlan looked up. "What did you say?"

"I think I have an easier way to do this. What if we dug a hole at the other end of the pipe by the house, cut the pipe off and then just pulled it out?"

All three men jammed their shovels into the ground and leaned on them.

"You have to be kidding." Wide-shouldered, ruddy-faced Harold smirked.

"No, I'm not." Jim looked Harold in the eye. "I saw them do something like that one summer when I worked in the oil fields in Illinois."

Harlan's eyebrows shot up and then they drew back down and together.

Paul pulled a handkerchief from his pocket, lifted his cap and wiped his brow. He looked from Harlan to Harold. "Why not try it? We have to dig the trench anyway. Two can dig a hole by the house, while the other two continue here."

The men all nodded in agreement.

119

Harlan climbed out of the trench and Jim got his shovel. They started a new hole just a few feet from the front door.

Within a half hour, they had enough of the pipe exposed to cut through it. Paul and Harold cut the pipe at the end of their trench.

Harold and Paul pulled on the pipe. It bent up a little, but it did not move through the ground.

"Maybe, we need a better grip. I'll get gloves out of the garage for us," Harlan said.

The men all put on gloves and grabbed the pipe.

Harlan said, "On three. Okay?"

The men nodded.

"One. Two. Three."

All four men strained together. Nothing moved.

Jim stood up and looked at the pipe and mumbled, "This should work. Let me think about what is wrong here."

Harlan looked at his sweaty friends and said, "Let's all think together. I will get us each a beer to drink while we think."

The men sat in the shade, holding their cold bottles of beer. They looked at the pipe. None of them wanted to dig the entire trench; they all wanted Jim's plan to work.

Jim gulped his beer.

"Let me work on this a few minutes," he said, standing up.

The other men were surprised when Jim didn't pick up his shovel. Instead, he walked to a shady spot by the house, lay down and pulled his cap over his eyes. They sipped their beers slowly, while Jim worked.

In ten minutes, Jim sat up, smiling smugly.

"I know what I forgot. We need to turn the pipe, to twist it in the ground."

He walked over to the pipe and tried to turn the end of it. Nothing happened.

Harlan put his gloves on and helped.

Harlan grimaced with the effort. Then, he grinned. "I feel it budging."

The others joined them. They turned it about one-quarter of the way. Then, they changed directions. It turned more easily the other way. They wiggled it back and forth a few times.

"Ready to pull?" Jim asked.

All four men tugged and the pipe slipped a little.

"Stop!" Harlan said. "We have to figure a way to hook the new pipe on or we will have to dig a trench for the new pipe!"

Together, they figured out how to connect the new pipe onto the old one and pulled it through. The job was done before nightfall.

That day, three tradesmen learned about physicists' work!

Brains work even when the eyes are closed!

Don't Put Two Seeds in a Pot

In mid-February, near Jim's birthday, I joined the legions of gardeners who plant seeds indoors, planning to transplant them in their gardens as soon as spring truly arrives. Since Jim died, I don't plant two seeds in each pot anymore.

I used to prepare pots with a special planting mix. Then, to ensure that each pot would have a viable plant for my garden, I put two seeds in each pot. If both of them sprouted and poked out of the soil, I would watch the plants for a few days, judge which seemed stronger, then snip the top of the weaker one at ground level. Until Jim's death, that seemed like a sensible way to prepare plants for my garden.

When I started pinching off the plants the spring after Jim died, I wondered if the remaining plant felt like I did without Jim. I imagined their roots entwined and sharing the moisture and nutrients in the soil. I wondered if the untouched plant could feel the roots slowly shriveling next to her and feel the emptiness in the soil surrounding them. Soon the tiny skeleton of the larger roots would melt away. Even though I told myself that the plant I had selected to grow to maturity would grow larger and be more productive alone, on that day I thought the plant might have preferred to be stunted and have smaller and fewer flowers than to be alone.

I know that it is illogical, but I'll never plant two seeds in the same pot again. I don't want to be reminded of my loneliness as I garden. Anyway, my loss of Jim was different.

Jim and I were not two seedlings with promise; we were mature and had produced three grown children. We were more like two shrubs that grew in the same place, sharing the sun, rain and fertile soil. Passersby would think that we were one plant, our branches were so entwined with one another. The casual onlooker would not have realized that we were interdependent, sharing resources and memories and that we strengthened one another with loving admiration and attention. By supporting one another's growth, we became a beautifully shaped and vigorous plant.

Jim's death was as if the Master Gardener had cut him off at the point where he emerged from the ground. I remained rooted to the same spot, feeling terribly misshapen and lopsided. His roots cried out. For there was no plant waiting for nutrients, nor were those roots receiving the gifts brought by sunlight. My roots touched his and misery flowed through me. I held his roots with mine and waited for the Master Gardener to finish his work. When he removed Jim's roots, I would be ripped from the earth with him.

The Master Gardener removed the portion of the shrub above the soil. In my pain, I didn't notice the gentleness with which the Master Gardener separated Jim's branches from mine. The Master Gardener had painstakingly and delicately untwisted the twigs and overlapping leaves one by one and, by degrees, withdrew Jim. Jim had been with me for so long and we had grown so used to one another's presence that I had stopped distinguishing his parts from mine long ago. How could the Master Gardener know which branches were his and which were mine when I couldn't feel the difference myself? I was stretched, pulled, twisted and nearly broken as the probing and unwinding proceeded tenderly, yet relentlessly. When we were finally separated, I felt bruised, battered and disoriented. My sense of self was distorted and diminished.

Shocked and exposed, I was surprised that I was still upright. My sheltering other's support no longer bolstered and encouraged me. Because of Master Gardener's deliberate carefulness though, my branches had no visible wounds oozing the grief that penetrated my entire being. Although my limbs were extraordinarily heavy without my helpmate beside me, they surprisingly did not sag or break. Searing sun pierced its way to my center and the winds whipped my branches without Jim's protection. I was fastened to the earth and our roots clung to it.

My feelings of loss kept me from appreciating the Master Gardener's foresight. Our branches had been untangled while Jim's were still supple, before they became stiffened with his death. Although I missed my companion and Jim's untiring support, I was still whole and functional. But in my distress, I did not know that.

The Master Gardener never did remove the roots. My memories of Jim are intact. Sometimes I cling to them, freezing them in my memory like the woody roots of the shrub.

Passersby noticed that my branches grew that first summer. Without his branches and leaves, I reached out trying to protect my and Jim's roots from the sun. Like all plants, I strived for symmetry and balance. My roots still cling to Jim's roots, but, under the surface, they were growing, too. Jim's roots were slowly becoming part of the soil and providing nourishment for my roots; he is being absorbed into my being.

Eventually, I noticed that the plants near us also missed Jim's shelter. They, too, had grown under his guardianship and were exposed to the parching sun and buffeted by the winds. My branches could only offer them limited cover. I noticed that they grew taller and stronger in response. At that time, I wondered if I, like my seedlings, might eventually grow to be a stronger plant without my companion. Or, was I too mature to tolerate this assault?

In due time, with the Master Gardener's skilled thoroughness, I became strong and healthy. I am whole.

Slowly, feelings of loss and incompleteness no longer visited me every day. I realized that I was resilient and cherished. My branches retained "our" shape, became stronger, reached up toward the sun, stretched out to our loved ones and embraced life. Gloriously, blossoms reappeared carrying promises of future fruit.

Now that I am a single plant where two once grew, I have stretched beyond the compact dense shrub Jim and I once were. It began with my desire to shelter our seedlings. Yet, they didn't need my protection; they were stretching upwards themselves. We all responded to the new conditions by growing. The stress was temporary. The Master Gardener provided the ingredients for growth and we began the change. A tree-like nature began to emerge. Our roots are going deeper and stretching into a wider circle; our crowns reach higher. Tall and resilient, we honor our benefactor.

Someday casual strangers won't realize the trauma I once suffered. They'll see the vigorous, productive plant I've become – but my branches will remember where Jim's branches once entwined mine. My limbs will always remember how Jim encouraged me to grow with him. Passersby may look carefully and see the negative space once reserved for Jim's branches. That negative space adds to the beauty, grace and mystery of my being.

The Master Gardener notices my old and new branches and sees the "we" that grew me.

I still don't plant two seeds in the same pot in the spring.

I'm Not Afraid to Die

"Momma."

Jean waited two heartbeats, and then repeated her plaintive call again. "Mommm-ma."

Jean was restless. A longing nagged at her. Maybe her mother's comforting embrace would put her at ease.

She gathered her strength and rose from her bed. Leaning against the wall, she shuffled room to room, calling for her mother.

Jean was near the end of her life but the loving connections to her friends and family were still strong. Even though her body had shriveled to skin and bones and she was so weak that talking exhausted her, her hugs poured out her indomitable loving spirit.

The nurse in Jean tried to mitigate the changes in her body, because she knew her loved ones needed her to be comfortable. She asked her nursing friends what dying would be like. They only knew about what happened to the body. Jean wanted to know about the threshold between life in her body and heaven. She was a Christian and believed in the heaven of her faith, but that didn't satisfy her need for a roadmap to the next world.

Curiosity and concern for her loved ones marked Jean's life. When she was told that the bothersome discomfort in her abdomen was ovarian cancer, Jean could imagine many more possibilities than the average person. For every frightening scenario she conjured up, Jean had a dose of hope. The balm of wishful scenarios tempered the moments of despair that threatened to strangle her confidence. Jean was determined not to allow cancer to suck any love from her life.

She turned to her friends and colleagues, including me, for help and advice. Her first two questions were: "What treatments are most likely to stop this cancer?" and "What can I do to make it easier for my family if I were to die?" Thus, Jean began the first of many cycles of treatment followed by remission followed by recurrence and treatment again.

She wrote love letters to her husband Darrell, their two daughters, her grandchildren, her parents and his parents. She marked items to be given to her daughters and grandchildren, and then made a video showing the objects and explaining their significance. The video was a love letter combined with words of wisdom. As she completed each task, she hoped that this work would become outdated and she would need to repeat it in a few years. This work was her legacy of love.

Jean had several periods of remission. Sadly, during one of those periods Darrell's father became ill and died. During another one, Jean's father also died after an illness. Jean thought it was miraculous that she was in remission, enabling her and Darrell to care for their fathers during the last months of their lives.

In addition, Jean's mother slipped into dementia after she was widowed. Jean and her brother placed their beloved Momma in a bright, clean nursing home with a caring and professional staff. Jean and Darrell took her mother for weeklong vacations in their home. Momma was visiting when this incident happened.

"Momma, there you are." Jean said, finding her mother staring vacantly out the kitchen window. "Momma, would you lie down with me? Just hold me for a while?"

Jean's mother turned around smiling into her daughter's eyes. She outstretched her arms.

Jean held her mother's hand and together they scuffled back to her bedroom. They lay down, her mother curling herself around Jean and wrapping Jean in her arms, in the same way she had when Jean was a toddler. Jean's restlessness seeped away and she fell into a deep sleep.

Jean found herself in an indescribably bright light place. She had never felt as loved as she did in this place. She knew what being loved felt like, but this was without bounds, with no beginning and no end. She settled into a state of incredible peace and happiness. She knew that this serene, absolute love was the Presence of God. It felt so good, so right, so intimate.

"Jean," Darrell shouted. "Oh, no. Jeannie, don't leave me now. Jeannie!"

Darrell responded to her mother's frightened guttural call. He ran into the room. Instantly, he understood. The mother and daughter on the bed. The tranquil expression on Jean's face. Her peaceful aspect. And she wasn't breathing.

Darrell scooped Jean's frail body into his arms and cradled her close to his chest, as if he were comforting a small child crying from a great hurt. He moaned and rocked side to side. He was the one who needed comfort. His whole being ached from losing her. His heartstrings tangled around Jean's body.

"Jeannie," he whimpered. "Jeannie, don't leave."

Jean heard the call and knew she had to leave the peaceful place. She had one more job to do. She breathed deeply.

Eyes closed, Darrell put his cheek next to hers.

"Jean," he sighed. "Thank God."

Jean kissed Darrell's ear.

"I have to tell you where I've been," she whispered. "I want you to call Pastor Pat."

When their minister arrived, Jean, Darrell, and her mother were outdoors bathed in the warm springtime sunlight. Darrell rubbed Jean's feet while she told them again about her journey to God's place. Pastor Pat took notes, and then read them back to Jean.

Jean smiled and patted the man's hand. Pointing her finger at the notes, she said, "I want you to read these for the sermon at my funeral. I want my friends and family to know what awaits me—and them. I want you to tell them that I said, 'You don't have to wait for the second coming. You can have it now.'"

This incident is why Jean's friends and family received an email from Darrell. It said: "Jean will die very soon. She is at peace with it."

Jean died a week later. She didn't need a roadmap; she knew the destination. It comforted her to be able to tell her loved ones about the love-filled place in the next life.

Jean's message changed the way I view life. I was confident that Jean told the truth. I began to see living here differently. Slowly, the belief that His Kingdom could be found here on earth seeped into my consciousness. I searched for ways that I could bring His Kingdom into my world.

When my heart was ready, I found a group of people dedicated to recognizing God's presence in their daily lives. At St. Bonaventure's, Jean's seed is growing and producing fruit.

I'm thankful that Jean came back and gave us the Good News. Her story erased any fear that I might have about the next life.

WISDOM TOO LATE

Life is one long experiment
in learning.
Who can be perfect all the time?
Sometimes I feel half-wise,
sometimes half-stupid.

~Terri Guillemets

Coulda Been a Millionaire

Jim stopped swinging his right arm and laid the sickle on the ground when I approached. Putting both hands on his knees, he rose from his stooped position. "There has to be an easier way to chop these weeds."

"I thought you might like to take a short break. It won't be long before lunch." I said.

"Whew! It sure is hot out here." Jim swiped the sweat from his brow with the back of his arm.

Smiling, he reached for the glass of ice water in my hand. "Thanks. How did you know that's what I was wishing for?"

I looked at the once knee-high wilting weeds lying at my feet. "How's your arm doing? Mine always gets tired slugging the sickle through tough weeds like those."

"I wish there was an easier way," he repeated, taking another sip and looking at the weeds that still needed chopped.

I looked toward the sickle. "Maybe the blade needs sharpening"

"Hmm. Where is the file?" Jim grinned sheepishly. He must have seen the spots of rust, too.

The ice cubes clattered in the glass and Jim handed it back to me.

"Lunch'll be ready in about a half hour. Do you think you'll have that area shorn by then?" I said over my shoulder.

I caught a glimpse of Jim's furrowed brow and a stiffening of his lips. Was Jim about to change from active work to his thinking mode? Or, was he just remembering where to find the file?

The kitchen felt cool and shadowy after the bright spring sunshine. I began to gather the ingredients for lunch. While I honed my knife, I heard the rhythmic tinny drag of the file against the sickle's blade.

Jim was quiet during lunch. *Is he that tired?* I thought. *Or, is he thinking?*

As if he'd read my thoughts, he said, "I've been thinking and I think I have a better way to cut those weeds. I bet if you could spin a foot-long piece of fishing line around fast enough, it'd cut the weeds."

I laughed. "Oh, Jim, how could a strand of flimsy nylon cut stuff that a sharp metal blade doesn't always chop down? Let's say you can make the line spin fast, wouldn't it just knock the weeds down?"

Jim wouldn't give up. "I'm sure it would work. And if I put it on a stick of the right length, you wouldn't have to bend down either.

"Think of how much safer it would be, too. No blade that could swing around and hit your legs. I always worry that I might cut a kid who pops up at the wrong time."

"That doesn't make sense," I replied. "If this thing could cut the grass, what would keep it from cutting through your trousers and hurting your shins?"

I thought that the topic was closed when Jim rose to return to the yard work.

About five years later, Jim called to me from the living room. "Janie, come here! Quick! You have to see what's on the TV. Hurry! They're showing my invention. They're using fishing line to cut weeds. It's working just like I said it would."

A man was holding a device about 48 inches long with a handle at one end and a motor about the size of a large can of beans at the other. As he moved the motor end along some tall plants, they laid down on the ground, like soldiers being mown down by a volley of gunfire. The man moved the motor around a pole with a fringe of grass and the grass disappeared. He turned the device off and a close-up showed plastic fishing line hanging from the bottom of it. The announcer touted the safety of the device, which he called a Weed Whacker.

"I could have been a millionaire," Jim sighed.

What if I hadn't discouraged him? How many other great ideas have been squashed by well-meaning "reality checks?"

Everything Comes Full Circle?

At some point, as if on command, the boomerang would make a wide arcing turn and return to the man's hand.

Our group was enthralled by his demonstration outside the Exploratorium. Over and over, the man hurled his boomerang into the air. Sometimes, he'd take a step forward or to a side to catch it, but mostly it returned to his outstretched hand.

Jim noticed how our nephew Doug smiled each time the man made the catch.

Jim grinned and spoke low enough that only I could hear. "Just wait until he sees the exhibits inside. The Exploratorium makes science seem magical but methodical. The kids will be touching and testing, not watching, like this."

Inside the kids pulled each other from one exhibit to the next. Sometimes, we adults needed to read and explain the directions, but usually they figured out what to do from watching the other visitors.

Near the end of the visit, Jim left the group, but rejoined them at the door. He handed the bag he was carrying to Doug. "Here's something to remember today by."

Doug opened the bag and pulled out a boomerang.

"I got it from the store inside. The next time our families get together, I bet you'll be able to throw the boomerang as good as the man today."

When we next visited Doug's family, he didn't demonstrate his boomerang skills.

Instead his mother Peggy showed us the four muntin window panes without glass. She pointed to the backyard which was almost the length of a football field saying:

"Doug was practicing with his boomerang in the back yard. He wanted to show you his progress. He has been having a hard time throwing it any distance.

"I heard a crash out here on the sunporch. The boomerang went through these windows!

"Doug came running and ran in the door, 'Mom, could you see if the boomerang was starting to turn?'"

"Can you believe that he had so much confidence that he threw the boomerang at the house and then believed that it would be turning back to him, even after it broke the windows?"

Not all things come full circle when we want them to.

Talent Search

"Use your God-given talents!" teachers exhorted us. But they didn't tell us what our talents were. If we have talents at birth, why don't we get labels or instructions telling us what they are?

When I stopped teaching at Wee Care, the parents pointed out a talent that I wasn't aware of.

Wee Care was a special time and place for me. I felt like I was doing the work I was born to do there. Hedy, Mary Ann, Cathie, Janice, Terri and I created an environment where a child's nature could unfold and grow. I watched children and their parents become confident, grow intellectually and truly care for one another.

Unfortunately, I wasn't taking a big enough salary home from the school. Lisa was in college, Lynda would enter college the next year and Dan wasn't far behind. We needed to educate our own children.

Jim found an ad in the newspaper wanting someone with backgrounds in nursing, teaching and computers. Not many people have that combination. That's how I became the nurse in Valley Memorial Hospital's computer department.

I was surprised and disappointed. In fact, I was in tears driving to school to tell my staff that I would no longer be at Wee Care. I was angry, too. I actually hollered in the car at God,

"I thought I was doing your work. I thought you'd help me find the money we need for our kids' college. Now I have to tell my staff that we have to close the school and let the children and parents down. Why?"

Then a thought so strong, it was like I was hearing a voice said, "Go ask your staff."

I didn't have the presence of mind to say, "Ask them what?"

Instead I presented the predicament to Mary Ann, Janice and Terri. Within 24 hours they had a plan worked out. Thanks to them Wee Care lasted another twenty years. And the three of them were the teachers there until the last day.

My last days at Wee Care as a teacher were bittersweet. Parents took the time to compliment me on my work there. I was perplexed because they didn't mention my science curriculum or any of the other areas I had worked so hard to develop. Instead they talked about how I listened to the children, how I comforted an unhappy child, and how I seemed to see the best in their children. They were talking about something inside me, not something I had learned studying Early Childhood Education. The parents gave me the first glimpse into how talents appear to the person with the talent.

My rule of thumb for recognizing talents that arose from that experience is: When someone asks you how you did something and you find it hard to give them the steps you took, you probably used a talent.

Searching for talents can take a lifetime, but I've found a shortcut—Gallup's StrengthsFinder program. Having seen the short-lived popularity of other tests and programs, I try to find ways to test their accuracy. For StrengthsFinder, I took the test twice. I also took a class on becoming a Strengths Coach. This system rang true.

The program teaches that talents become strengths through use, like building muscles through exercise. It also promotes strengthening talents, rather than remediating weaknesses.

In coaching people about their top five strengths, I found that people often found it especially difficult to recognize their top two strengths. They often told me, "Isn't that the way everyone does things?" For them, using talents is intuitive and natural. When they received the results from the StrengthsFinder test they began to consciously use their talents and understand that other people had other "natural" approaches.

My top two talents are: Learner and Connectedness. The other three are: Responsibility, Strategic and Maximizer. You'll see them played out in this book.

Being a learner, I am never quite finished with a subject. There always seems to be a little more to be learned. My science project is an example of continuing to learn from an experience.

Those of us with the learner talent tend to use our own experiences as a jumping-off point for further learning. I've haven't been as interested in professional or academic credentials as the learning itself. (Could that be the reason for the varied careers?)

My curiosity has sparked my interest in traveling, studying, reading, gardening and other activities.

People with Connectedness believe that things happen for a reason. I know that we are all connected and part of something bigger than ourselves. The stories given to me that appear in *Glimpsing Across the Threshold* reinforced my feeling of connectedness.

My third talent of Responsibility was one of the three characteristics in Dad's Three Rules for Success. No wonder I made that rule my own.

I often used my Strategic Talent to find the easiest way to do things. Before the test, I thought I naturally took the lazy way. Maximizers can make a silk purse from a sow's ear.

Everyone has a unique blend of talents, but they have to discern them themselves.

MY WORLD CHANGES

Experience is a hard teacher
because she gives the test first,
the lesson afterward.

Vernon Law

My Name Changes

I can understand how the people in the Middle Ages thought that sailors could go too far in uncharted waters and fall off the edge of the world. Because that's how I felt on my first day of school.

Until that day, my parents were always within the range of my voice. I had never been any farther from my parents than the grass that surrounded our house. We had never even had a babysitter. When we went to the grocery store or church, Mom or Dad was with us. Going to visit one of Mom or Dad's brothers or sisters, who lived on farms surrounding the town of Vincennes in southern Indiana, was a big Sunday outing. Everywhere I went, I saw the familiar faces that I'd seen all my life.

As the September of my fifth year approached, my mother's uneasiness unsettled me. The time for me, the firstborn, to go to school was imminent. Mother paid unusual attention to my appearance, particularly my wardrobe.

I heard her ask my aunts, "What kind of outfits do girls wear to school?"

"Dresses," they told her.

Mom sewed "school dresses" for me.

Before the summer ended, Mom also took me to town to buy a new pair of black leather never-wear-out shoes from Grundman's Shoe Store, along with their specially formulated thick black shoe polish.

Finally, the morning of my first day of school arrived. It felt like a Sunday Mom washed, groomed and dressed me and my sister N'ellen and brother Henry, like we were going to church. Mom put on her Sunday dress, too. Then she put us all in the Chevy and turned from our cinder lane to the oiled gravel road to the two-lane highway that led to Bruceville's only school, a square brick two-story building that looked even bigger than our country church.

Mom helped us get out of the car, saying, "Watch out for the school buses. N'ellen, hold my hand. Janie, you'll have to hold N'ellen's hand because I have to carry Henry. We're going to figure out which bus'll bring Janie home."

Mom knew that I'd be riding a bus to school and back to the farm each day. I don't know how Mom determined that the neighboring children rode on "Route 2" or how she knew who the children were.

To me, the buses all looked the same, yellow with black designs on them. When the door on the side of the bus opened, children who seemed much bigger and noisier than me stepped down the two steps onto the crunchy white limestone gravel and hurried away in all directions.

When one of the buses was nearly empty, my mom shepherded all three of us kids toward a tall girl with long blonde braids who had just stepped out of the bus.

Stepping in front of the girl, Mom asked, "Are you one of the Steimel girls who live in the brown house by Bob Hill's place?"

The girl nodded her head affirmatively, somewhat shyly.

"Isn't your little brother starting first grade this year?"

Again the girl's head bobbed up and down.

Pointing to me, my mother said, "This is my daughter who's also starting the first grade. I'm Mary Holscher and we live on Bob Hill's farm. Could you make sure she gets on your bus when school's out?"

Another bobbing of the head and the girl ran into school.

Then, Mom turned to me and said, "Remember that girl. When school is out, I want you to find her. Understand?"

I must have nodded my head or assented somehow, because Mom moved us toward the building's double-doored mouth.

We joined the stream entering the building. Mom kept asking people, "Which way to the First Grade Room?"

I clung to N'ellen's hand, afraid that I might get lost. All the while, I looked for familiar faces, expecting a cousin or aunt or uncle to come around a corner or walk down the hall and beam a smile of recognition. All I could see were the shoulders, arms and feet of strange children who were all taller than me. We reached the door of my classroom without me seeing any relatives.

Mom led us into a huge room with blackboards along the wall. In the middle of the room, there were six wooden tables, each with six child-size wooden chairs.

Five and six-year-olds accompanied by their mothers were lined up along the blackboard. A woman sat at a desk in front. The mother at the front of the line went to the desk with at least one child in tow and talked to the woman. The woman asked, listened and wrote.

I searched for a familiar face in the line, but I only knew my mom and my siblings!

Finally, we were at the front of the line. Mrs. Flossy had a clean white index card and she held her pen expectantly. "Last name?" She said.

"Holscher," Mom said.

"First name?"

"Janet."

I stood quietly holding to Mom's skirt, peeking at the Mrs. Flossy's warm gray eyes. I didn't understand the terms "lass-names" and "firs-names."

When they finished talking, Mrs. Flossy looked at me and said, "Glad to meet you, Janet."

I was confused, but my mom took me to a table, told me to sit down, and went out the door with N'ellen and Henry.

At that moment, I fell off the edge of my known world! Mom wouldn't hear me if I called. I was with strangers in an uncharted building with unusual customs. They didn't even know to call me Janie. I was in a daze and drifted through the day. I didn't smile, but I didn't cry either.

Finally, the girl that my mom told me to remember came to the door of our classroom. She took a boy by the hand. Then, she looked around the room until she saw me looking at her. She smiled and, still holding the boy's hand, walked over to me. She reached out for my hand and took the boy and me out of the classroom.

I held her hand tightly as we wandered through the maze of halls.

We stood momentarily on the steps outside the building's door. The girl looked down the steps to the bus parking lot. There were five bright yellow buses.

Will she choose the right bus? I worried.

Confidently, the girl with long blonde braids walked toward the buses. She stopped beside one of the buses and pointed to a squiggly mark on the side of the bus.

"See this?" she asked.

"This is the number two. Our bus is the only bus with this number. That's how you will know this is our bus. Now, let's get on the bus."

First, the boy stomped up the black steps. Then, me. Finally, the big girl.

"Sammy, see that empty seat back there?" the girl asked the boy.

The boy smiled that he knew which seat.

"Sit down there, Sammy. Janet, you, too. I'll sit on the aisle."

When children stopped getting on the bus, the driver closed the door, started the engine and drove away from the school. Occasionally, the bus stopped, some children stood up, the driver opened the door and the children stepped down the two steps onto the road.

Eventually, when the bus stopped, the girl took Sammy and me to the front of the bus. She said something to the driver and he opened the door. Instead of taking me with her and Sammy, she said, "Janet, stay on the bus. Sit in this seat right behind Mr. Morris. Your house is the next stop. Mr. Morris told me that he'll make sure you get off there." Then, they were gone.

I sat absolutely still. The stiff upright feeling that had been inside my chest all day was getting stiffer.

The next stop was by our mailbox. I stood up, the driver opened the door, and I stepped out to our lawn.

Like the ancient mariners, I didn't fall off the edge of the world, never to return home. My mother's foresight had ensured my return. I came back from a world populated by strangers who didn't know me or my family.

The stiff armor that had encircled my chest all day broke loose and I felt free to smile, wave my arms and twirl around. I was in Janie's homeland again.

Each weekday thereafter, Janie boarded the #2 bus, was Janet at school, and returned to Janie's world each afternoon. Thus, began my exploration and charting of territories beyond my home and family.

Since my first day of school, my name has marked the fluctuating boundary between my family and the outside world. I was given the name Janet, whose sound pleased my mother's ears, on the day I was born. Dad almost immediately began calling me, "my little Janie." I was called Janie at home and at family gatherings for a long time. But, gradually, during my grade-school and high-school years, the borderlines of my name blurred. I was Janet at school and, with time, my brothers and sisters, as well as some of my aunts, uncles and cousins, began to call me Janet, too.

When I entered high school, my class of 37 young women included three cousins. They initiated the reclamation of my original name. They called me Janie, although my teachers and other classmates knew me as Janet. When they called me Janie, feelings of security, gentleness and self-assurance welled up. I liked the way Janie felt.

In school I had learned that the world is round. Instead of falling off an edge, we can circle round to the starting point. I repossessed my first name Janie when I entered nurses' training. As a nurse, I combined the knowledge and scientific nursing process I learned at St. Mary's School of Nursing with the compassion and intuition I had learned from my family.

The borderlines of my name blurred and slowly reversed. I was Janie at school. My brothers and sisters began to call me Janie. Former classmates from grade school and high school still thought I was Janet.

When I married Jim, my last name changed from Holscher to Eddleman. Jim and I moved to California a few months after our wedding. Our new friends knew me only as Janie. I had almost succeeded in integrating the warmth of a being a treasured child into my entire life. Only bureaucrats, like the bank and the Internal Revenue Service, address me as Janet.

Whether I am called Janie or Janet, Mom or Grandma, Wife or Friend, I try to respond with the simplicity and trust that my gentle, shy five-year-old self felt before the first day of school.

Three Year Reign Ends

The house was atwitter with excitement. Ten eyes were peering out the window hoping that the '55 blue Chevy would appear around the bend in the lane. We couldn't sit still and moved from window to window, hoping to be the first to see them. Dad had left an hour before to get Mom from the hospital. The house was tidy and we were all dressed in clean clothes with our hair neatly combed, but we still looked for more ways to make our home feel welcome. We checked that the bed was ready for Mom again and again. Occasionally, someone would brave the uncharacteristically crisp October air to step outside to look for a blue fender emerging from behind the big barn.

Nell was the one who yelled, "They're coming! They're at the turn by the workshop."

We threw the doors open and stood shivering on the front porch, watching the car drive along the horse pasture, making the last turn at the rosebushes, then passing the five maple trees and, finally, reaching the end of our lane. The familiar sound of the tires on cinders came to a halt.

Dad stepped out and circled around the back of the car to open Mom's door. Mom right foot tentatively touched the ground and she turned in her seat, holding a bundle of blankets in her arms. She carefully walked across the lawn sprinkled with daffodil-yellow maple leaves. Her eyes wrapped us each in her smile as she climbed the three wooden porch steps.

Right there on the porch, even before Mom entered the house, we were jostling to hold the bundle. Nell took the little bundle as soon as Mom crossed the threshold into her and Dad's bedroom. Nestling the bundle close to her, Nell lowered herself into the child-sized wooden rocking chair. She smiled at the bundle and, purring gentle words, lifted a corner of the soft, creamy blanket. Everyone tiptoed around Nell, trying to find a place where they could see the little scrunched up face. Hands reached out gently touching the miniature fist. Kathy, my fourth little sister and sixth sibling, was thus welcomed into the heart of our family. We each wanted to hold her in our arms and personally meet her.

Well, to be honest, not everyone wanted to touch and behold this new little one. I noticed my three-year-old sister Anita standing outside the circle of baby adorers. I must have looked as puzzled as Anita did. At first I couldn't understand her look of naked confusion, as her eyes, beneath her questioning brow, darted from person to person. A minefield seemed to stretch between her circle of aloneness and the tightly knit group paying homage to the infant. Her round face projected thoughts of *Why aren't they watching me? I talk. I walk. I am the cute one.* She seemed about to cast a ribbon of tears out to the throng of baby worshipers.

My heart went out to Anita. I thought, *She looks so hurt, almost ready to cry.*

All of the times that she had been at my side this summer flashed through my mind. When Anita couldn't keep up with us kids, she had allowed me to pick her up and carry her on my right hip, holding her in place with my right arm. In this way, she had accompanied me when I picked green beans, pulled sweet corn or harvested hills of new potatoes. She had deigned to let me carry her up the lane to the workshop to get Dad for dinner many times. On my hip, Anita had expanded her kingdom beyond the house and backyard.

I thought, *Why am I over here? Hadn't she almost been attached to my right hip this summer?*

So, I disentangled myself from the baby crowd and joined Anita. I gathered her into my twelve-year-old arms, lifted her, put her on my right hip and waded into the circle around the baby so that Anita could see the cause of the excitement.

"See her hands?" I commented. "They look almost too small to have fingernails, don't they? Look how much bigger your hands are. Isn't the baby's face tiny? It is almost like your doll's face. Her name is Kathy. Oh, look at her squirm. Did you see her stick her tongue out?"

Slowly Anita's curiosity supplanted her uncertainty. I noticed, but did not mention, that although two arms of a sibling encircled Kathy, two hands of a parent supported the infant.

Mom reclaimed Kathy and laid her on their double bed and slowly unwrapped the coverings for all of us to see the newest family member. I placed Anita on the bed next to the edge of Kathy's outer blanket. Anita lay on her stomach and watched until Mom revealed Kathy's miniature fingers and toes. Anita reached out and touched Kathy's right hand. Someone snapped a photo as Anita paid homage to the new queen of the household.

I didn't hold Kathy until much later in the day. I was more concerned with Anita's feelings. In a childlike way, I sensed that she needed support to fill the vacuum left by the sudden loss of the family's focus. Besides, there wasn't much competition for Anita's attention; everyone was more concerned with touching and holding the newest sovereign.

I wonder if I was acting out of my own unmet needs when my sister Nell entered our home for the first time. Had crossing the gap between reigning baby to not-youngest been as painful for me? Had I felt anything similar when Henry, the first son, was born? When Betty Jo was born, I *was* six years old and surely had moved into the role of caregiver. Could I have misinterpreted Anita's behavior?

Ever since that time though, I made a special effort to be near my youngest sibling when the next three babies were introduced to our family. I was always prepared to coddle the not-so-young one. Who could better comfort a regent who has abruptly lost their throne than someone who was once a queen herself?

Locks and Keys

I grew up in a lock-free world on a farm about three miles outside of Vincennes, Indiana. Doors and windows didn't need latches or fasteners to keep pesky critters and inclement weather out. Visitors always knocked and waited to be invited into our home. Keys were left in the car's ignition, ready for any of our family's drivers. This way of life was threatened in 1956 by a person we had never met when Leslie Irvin escaped from jail.

My mother learned of the escape from our landlady Mrs. Ewing, who telephoned and said, "Mary, Mad Dog Irvin has escaped from jail. He might be coming this way. Get all the kids inside and lock all your doors. Make sure Bub's gun is loaded and ready."

"Are you sure?" Mom asked. "Isn't he in that escape-proof jail in Princeton?"

"Mary, there is no time to talk. Do what I say! The man is loose. You know he goes after isolated farm families, like us. Lock up your house now." Mom sat the phone back in its cradle, her eyes narrowed and face hardened, just like the time she killed the water moccasin in our yard with a hoe.

Leslie Irvin was creating havoc once again.

In 1955, the panic that swept through the area didn't have a name yet. It began when the four adult members of the Duncan family were found shot in the head with their hands bound behind their backs on their family farm in Henderson County, Kentucky. The description of a two-year-old girl, who was sitting beside her mother's dead body, whimpering, "Mommy is sleepy," troubled even the most hardened reader. Her grandmother, the elder Mrs. Duncan, was found in another bedroom still alive. Mrs. Duncan was rushed to the community hospital and an armed guard was posted outside her room.

As the news of these killings spread, the peace-loving pastoral community became a wary unwelcoming populace. Police warned against visiting friends and relatives unannounced. A local newspaper reported, "A woman, alone with six of her children at her home in Geneva, heard a knock on the door. She asked who was there. When there was no reply, she fired through the door." Likewise, a seed-corn salesman stopped making calls after being greeted at more than one door by a gun-wielding housewife. Gun and ammunition sales skyrocketed.

Police working around the clock to solve the triple murders found three similar murders near Evansville, Indiana in the preceding three months. Eleven days after the murders, Leslie Irvin, a 30-year-old construction worker, was arrested. He confessed to committing at least 27 burglaries and stealing three handguns. Although, at first, he denied any involvement in any murders, within two days he confessed to the Duncan murders and the other three Indiana murders. Before the end of the year, Leslie "Mad Dog" Irvin was convicted of murder and sentenced to death. Hoosiers returned to their neighborly ways again.

Then, in January 1956, Leslie Irvin escaped from the escape-proof jail in Princeton, only 25 miles from our home. Hysterical waves of panic ricocheted through southern Indiana and into our home with Mrs. Ewing's phone call.

Since it was January, all of us kids were already indoors. Mom got the key down from the hook in the closet. She had to twist and turn the key before it finally locked the door leading to their bedroom from the front porch.

When the key wouldn't work on the other door off the front porch, Mom's eyes brimmed with tears and she threw the key across the room. She probably was thinking, "Why even bother to try to protect ourselves with these flimsy locks, especially since neither of the two back doors have a lock?"

For the back doors, she could only hook the screen doors. We children moved from window to window looking for any movement outside.

I don't know if Mom loaded Dad's gun. When Dad came in from the fields that evening, we stopped our constant peering out the windows. Mad Dog Irvin wasn't as frightening with both Mom and Dad in the house. Our nervousness ebbed away and our usual sense of safety surfaced again.

Leslie Irvin became the subject of a nationwide search and was on the FBI's "Ten Most Wanted" list. Today he would be called a "serial killer." Less than three weeks after his escape, Mad Dog Irvin was found 2,000 miles away in San Francisco.

Mad Dog Irvin's effect on our family was extraordinarily short-lived. A key was never found for the lock on the other front door and locks were never put on the back doors. Car keys were still left in the ignition. The only intruders we guarded against were mosquitos and flies.

My world has changed in the fifty years since Leslie Irvin terrorized southern Indiana and Kentucky. I live in the suburbs of the San Francisco Bay area. The pesky critters I want to keep out are quite different than those of my rural childhood. Most of my windows in my house don't have screens because we don't have many flies, mosquitoes or other insects. Although neither I nor my neighbors have ever experienced a problem, I routinely lock my doors and windows to prevent illegal entries. I not only remove my keys from my car's ignition, I lock its doors, too. In Livermore, as in most urban areas, it is considered unneighborly not to take these protective measures.

Yet, when I return to Wonder Farm, my family's farm in Indiana, I step back fifty years. Mom and Dad's back door is unlocked. Theft is less threatening for my parents than being cut off from their family and neighbors. Like them, I leave the keys in the ignition of my rental car. I can grab my suitcase knowing that the back door's open. It feels comfortable returning to the freedom of that lock-free existence of rural life.

Returning to the Bay Area, I remind myself that there are all kinds of locks. Minds and spirits can be locked as well as doors and windows. I revel in the freedom of expression in the Bay Area. It's like a fresh spring breeze clearing out the stale air of a house that has been sealed all winter. I don't need screens to stop the flow of new ideas. Cultural diversity is welcome. The doors of my home may be locked, but my mind is open.

Flying the Coop

On the farm in Indiana, where I grew up, there was only one house within hollering distance and that was our landlord's home. It was about a city block away from our house. The lane to our houses meandered from the highway through The Woods. If we heard or saw a car, we knew they were coming to see us or the Ewings.

When I looked out the kitchen window while I washed dishes in the evening, I saw a pine tree silhouetted in the afterglow of the setting sun. We didn't need to draw the shades on our bedroom windows for privacy or to keep the light from the streetlights out. The lawn, trees and fields were our shutters.

Our home had three bedrooms for my parents and my three brothers and six sisters. Sometimes, I just wanted to be alone, and then I would walk out our back door and down the lane into my comforting place, The Woods.

The Woods was planted by the landlords' grandfather. Most of the trees were sugar maples, but there was a small grove of pecan trees. Scattered throughout The Woods were persimmons, firs, poplars, and oaks, but my favorite was a majestic beech tree with pooling of a small stream near its feet. Images of the sky, leaves and branches overhead were reflected on the surface, a small minnow swam in the water and the bottom was lined with fallen leaves. I felt free there and nourished by the outdoors.

When Jim and I moved to California, living in town, I felt as cooped up as one of my mother's chickens.

The hen house was a shed with one window and two doors. One door had a latch outside and we used it to bring in food and carry out eggs. Like prison guards, we had to be careful that no hens escaped. The hens had a door that was just a square hole big enough for one chicken at a time to go out to their yard. Like inmates, the hens' exercise yard was surrounded by a wire fence.

Caught in the city, I paced our apartment. When we moved into a house, I could open the back door and walk in its backyard. But a fence kept me in. There were no soothing woods beckoning me.

Occasionally, one of Mom's hens would escape the enclosure by flying over the fence. Usually, she walked back and forth near the fence calling to her friends. I thought she was saying, "How do I get back in? I miss you gals."

Those escapees weren't very hard to catch. Before putting the hen back in the hen house, my mother would clip the feathers of one wing with a pair of old scissors, making the bird out of balance and unable to fly over the fence until the feathers were replaced with new ones.

I felt as out of balance as one of those hens with clipped wings when we moved to the city. I looked out my windows and saw more windows. People in the city walked on pavement. I missed being able to take a long walk on the soft earth. I longed to walk all alone along the bank of a small trickling stream like the one at my childhood home in The Woods. All the streams I could walk along were in public parks and had a busy feeling. Wandering off the path was discouraged because it was either unsafe for me or for the environment.

After seven long years, I finally began to feel at ease in Livermore—or, at least, I was used to being cooped up. I decided that I could tolerate city life.

A few years ago, when I found a path in Veteran's Park that wanders into Sycamore Grove, I finally felt like I had escaped from the chicken yard. That dirt path, which sometimes draws near the creek and is often shaded by mature sycamore trees, makes me feel like I have finally flown the coop. I feel at home on the dirt trails where I can feel the contours of rocks and soil through thin soled shoes. The trees wrap me in their shadows. The old feelings of peace, trust in a better tomorrow, and freedom flood back. The grove's natural beauty and the conversations of the surrounding wildlife soothe my spirit.

Now that I've escaped into Sycamore Grove, I have been thinking about my mom's hens. Could the escapee have been giving a motivational speech to the hens still inside? Could she have been saying, "Come on, girls. Fly away with me."

Meeting Hedy

"That will be $21.17," the clerk said, looking at the total on the cash register, and then putting the final item in a large brown paper bag.

The woman worked with speed and precision. She had picked up the items, pushed the buttons on the cash register, and bagged the purchases with the coordination of an athlete. She knew the prices of almost all of the objects, only needing to look for the price tag on a tiny pink dress set.

While she waited for my husband to finish writing the check, the woman turned her attention to my infant daughter and me. Her eyes seemed to caress my baby's hand, which had slipped out of the soft flannel blanket, while she cooed, "What a cute baby girl." Then, looking up at me, she asked, "How old is she?"

The clerk seemed to be in her early twenties, like me. She was a little taller than me, about 5'5". She wore a neatly ironed shirt and slacks, also similar to mine. She had brown hair, too, but hers was cut like Audrey Hepburn's, short with wispy bangs. Her smile spread over her entire face, pulling everything upward – making tiny lines in her forehead, a hint of creases on the outer edge of her eyelids, rounding and tightening the flesh over her cheekbones, deepening her cheek where a dimple often is found on others, opening her lips and exposing a perfect row of white teeth. The smile wrapped my little Lisa and me in its sincerity.

I hadn't expected this kind of familiarity at a check-out line in Value Giant, a variety store located on First Street in Livermore. Jim and I often shopped in this precursor to K-Mart, which carried middle-class paraphernalia, like small appliances, sporting equipment, clothing, and household goods.

"I wish I could reach out to strangers, like her," I thought.

As I unwrapped Lisa's blanket to show her dimpled elbows to the friendly woman, I felt the shell that surrounds my family soften a little.

"She's three weeks old," I said. "Her name is Lisa." I held the little bundle out, within in the clerk's easy reach.

Oblivious to our conversation, Jim finished writing the check, tore it out of the checkbook and placed it in one of the clerk's hand, which was outstretched to stroke my baby.

She eyed the plain blue personal check Jim had just written, as if it could tell his fortune. Glancing up at Jim, she asked, "Do you go to Teller Tech?"

"Uh, yes," Jim replied with a surprised look on his face. "How did you guess that?"

The clerk tipped her head to the side, pleased with her deductive powers. Then, she looked from Jim to Lisa to me, spinning a web of intrigue around us.

There weren't many people in the store. It was early in the evening and most of Value Giant's potential customers were home eating supper. There was no one behind us in line and no one hurrying us to complete this transaction.

I wondered, *How did she reach that conclusion? Is it that obvious that Jim's a student there?*

I tucked Lisa's blanket around her. I felt the hastily constructed bridge of female comradeship collapsing.

"My husband is Irv Lindemuth," the woman said. "He's also a student at Teller Tech. He told me that a fellow student and his wife had a baby a couple of weeks ago and that they named her Lisa, like our daughter."

Her eyes sparkled and she laughed impishly, "I just took a chance that you might be the same ones. Why don't you come over for dinner tomorrow night and meet our daughter?"

The planks of a bridge of fellowship were falling back into place. "We would like that," I said. "Can I bring a dessert?"

The woman tore a strip from the cash register roll, picked up a ballpoint pen and began to write. At the same time, she said, "My name is Hedy. Here is our phone number and address. Will six o'clock be okay for you?"

In those few minutes, a stranger transformed our lives.

The Lindemuth and Eddleman families shared many holidays together. They went on camping trips. In fact, they built a network of mutual friends, who were among the "aunts and uncles" present at Lisa's wedding years later.

What if Hedy hadn't reached out to us that evening?

Cashing in on Family's Reputation

Have you heard the phrase *Everybody knows everybody in a small town*?

While I was cashing a personal check at a bank in my hometown, that adage was validated. It occurred in 1981 during one of the rare visits Jim and I made to Vincennes. In fact, we were making our fifth visit since marrying and moving to Livermore fifteen years before.

When I placed my personal check in the brushed chrome drawer of the drive-up window of the local bank, I was worried that the bank might refuse to cash it. I was from out of state. My friends and I had already had the experience of having the bank at the shopping mall twenty-five miles from Livermore refuse to cash checks because they were drawn on another bank or because we were from out of town. So, I craned my neck towards the microphone and said somewhat meekly, "You'll see that this check is from out of state. What kind of identification would you like?"

The teller peered at me from her perch behind the thick green-tinted window.

Oh, oh, I thought, *she's ready to reject my check. It'll be just like I told Mom it would be. Mom had laughed, but she had never tried to cash a check anywhere outside of Vincennes.*

I tried to steel myself for the impending humiliation.

The drawer closed and the teller picked up the check at her fingertips.

"Hmmm. Eddleman. From California," she said reading the identification on my check.

She peered out the window at me and asked, "Would you be that Holscher girl who married Charlie Eddleman's boy?"

"Yes," I replied.

"Enjoying your visit?" she asked.

I nodded and she continued, adding another statement or question before I could nod, shake my head, or answer her.

"Bet you brought your kids to see the grandparents.

"Have they caught any lightnin' bugs?

"Have you taken your kids to George Rogers Clark Memorial to sit in the giant's lap?

"Sure must be hot out there. Nice and cool in here. Come inside next time.

"Hope you enjoy your stay."

The drawer slid back to me with a stack of bills held down with a black rock.

"Thank you," I said, picking up the bills. "I can't see through the glass in this light. Do you mind if I ask who you are?"

"Mary Lou Cary. Your dad and my mom are third cousins."

"Thanks, Mary Lou," I said and rolled up my window.

I didn't know her and had never heard of her, but she knew how I was connected to the town. That's life in a small town. You'll be a "local" all your life, no matter how far away you roam.

Especially in small towns, a family's good reputation is a heritage that is passed down for generations.

MY HERITAGE

Tzadikim nistarim...is from Hasidic Jewish lore...at any given time there are a specific number of people who support the world, or maybe it's just a village. Their caring and righteousness are what keeps the village alive. Without them, we would perish. But here's the thing: they don't know that they are *tzadikim nistarim* because of their extraordinary humility and goodness. In fact, if people think that they might be members of the club, then that alone is proof that they are not. The world keeps turning because of them, we keep falling love, we keep having sweet babies, and we write books and make sculptures because of them. And they go unheralded.

Ira Levine, a character
in Jacqueline Sheehan's
[picture this]

Farm People

I am a daughter, granddaughter and great-granddaughter of farmers. I think that my whole family tree is populated by farmers. Even the ancestors that immigrated to Indiana from Germany were farmers, kotters to be exact.

Kotters lived on "kottens," which were farms rented from the lord. The right to rent the land was an inheritance passed on to the oldest son. Eventually the oldest son would move into the main house and the parents would be "retired" to a smaller house. The smaller the house the closer people lived to their animals. My ancestors lived under one roof with their beasts. In the bigger houses, there was a sliding door between the lines of stalls and the house. If the home was big enough a common area with a huge fireplace and long table was used by the family and hired help. That was where they worked, cooked, did laundry, etc. At the end of the communal area farthest away from the animals, the family might have a room or two.

I think these ancestors must have been like my father—a man of the land. I remember him reaching down with his right hand and scooping up a handful of soil. He would look at the color and texture. He'd sort of rub and sift the soil through his fingers. Then he would declare that it needed a little more manure, or

166

that it was getting better. Dad tended the soil and was proud of leaving any place he farmed better because of his care.

That is what my kind of farmers does. Even when the land isn't their own, they tend it and prepare it for the next generation. Maybe that came from all those generations who were kotters.

Grandma Halter

My most vivid impressions of Grandma Halter arise from my memories of afternoon visits on warm summer afternoons in her kitchen. She was my mother's mother and the memories are from their mother-daughter visits interrupted by our childish needs.

My feet remember her kitchen better than my eyes. My bare feet would carry the warm soft sandy feeling from the sparse lawn to the worn speckled linoleum floor. The murmur of the mother-daughter chat at the kitchen table was accompanied by the whirr of an oscillating fan, the purr of the freezer, and the tick-tock of the grandmother clock. The subdued sunlight filtered by the maple trees and the closed window shades highlighted the red checked curtains.

I think Grandma liked having children in her house. She kept a box of toys in her kitchen. It usually had one or two dolls and a couple of trucks that often were missing a wheel. Our favorite plaything was in a gold-colored tin box, whose lid opened to reveal paperless bits of bright colored crayons. When we brought the box to the oilcloth covered kitchen table, Grandma would find coloring books for us. After a while, she would set a bowl of candy by us. I still associate soft orange peanut shaped candies or nougats wrapped in cellophane with Grandma Halter and her kitchen.

Grandma's hair fascinated me. She was the only woman I knew who wore her hair pinned in a knot on the top of her head. I wondered how long her hair was. My mother told us how, as a child, she liked to watch Grandma groom her hair. Although I saw her comb, silver brush and thick gray pins on her dressing table, I never saw her use them. I imagined her bun being transformed into Rapunzel-thick hair cascading down her back when she released it from those pins.

Each year, Grandma Halter made something for each of her grandchildren. One year, every granddaughter received a doll clothed in a blue gingham dress, panties and scarf – all sewn by Grandma. I know Grandma made the dresses because I saw her show my mother the material and a sample doll.

Grandma Halter's house only had one flaw--her outhouse. It was inside a fenced chicken yard with a gate latch too high to be reached by a child. Booby traps of chicken droppings dotted the path to the outhouse. Forever on guard, a wily old rooster attacked any human intruders who were not wielding the big "rooster" stick that Grandma kept by the gate. I never felt old enough to go out there without an adult protector.

Grandma Halter died while I was in grade school. I never saw her when she was sick or confined to a bed. I didn't get to tell her, "Good-bye."

Sadly, in my memory Grandma Halter is as much a place as a person. I can't recall the sound of her voice or laughter, or how it felt to sit on her lap. But I can remember feeling welcome in her home. Her kitchen was a comfortable place, a sort of haven.

I use Grandma's recipe for dumplings to make one of my family's favorite meals of Roast Beef and Dumplings. Her impromptu frying of torn off lumps of leftover bread dough, which she coated with cinnamon sugar and named "Door

Knobs," has been a family treat for her children, me, my siblings, my children and my grandchildren.

My memories of Grandma Halter remind me of the importance of having toys for visiting children in my home.

Grandma Holscher

Using fragmented childhood memories to draw conclusions about the character of either of my grandmothers is no more reliable than determining the color of a faceted crystal from the specks of colored light projected on the wall. As my life experiences accumulate, I continue to reinterpret my memories. They are still shaping *my* character, just as my grandparents' genes inexorably influence my physical being.

When I was a youngster, all adults, including both Grandma Halter and Grandma Holscher, towered over me. The difference in our sizes receded as I grew older and eventually I was two inches taller than Grandma Holscher, but I'm still shorter than Grandma Halter was. About the time our heights intersected, I began to see Grandma Holscher as an individual with feelings, hopes and fears. With this new perspective, my estimation of her began to rise and still continues to heighten long after her death.

Grandma was a tidy little woman, who must have had boundless energy and determination. When we visited her home, everything was in order. The furniture stood at attention in its proper place. Beds were unwrinkled. Bath towels were folded and hung on towel racks. The stove gleamed and kitchen faucets sparkled. Dust never settled in Grandma's house and fingerprints almost disappeared before they alit on any shiny surface. When Grandma offered us a piece of candy, she always had a washcloth ready to whisk any lingering flavor or stickiness from our fingers.

When I was in the First Grade, Grandma Holscher became associated with the scent of bacon and speckled eggs. At that time, I was preparing for my First Communion and, each Sunday morning, our family drove the thirty minutes from Bruceville to St. Vincent's Parish in Vincennes, where many of Dad's family went to church. After Mass, some of them would stay and visit with my parents while I attended instructions. Usually, our family (Mom, Dad, me, Nell, Henry and baby Bet) went to Grandma and Grandpa's for breakfast afterwards. Even before Grandma opened her door, the wafts of bacon scent greeted us. Quickly, Grandma prepared platters of breakfast foods for us. Her bacon strips were thick, dark, and chewy. Her eggs were sprinkled with irregular flecks from the bacon drippings and had fringes of lacy brown crispness. Toast was piled high. Grandma would emerge from her kitchen and the apron tied at her waist would be spotless, her dress unwrinkled and her short gray hair neatly arranged.

These mornings were also marked by the absence of other cousins. If we had visited Grandma and Grandpa Holscher on a Sunday afternoon, usually one, two or more of Dad's siblings would also be there with their families. Since Grandma didn't have any toys at her house, the other youngsters were our source of entertainment. On the rare occasions when ours was the only family visiting, it was tedious to sit in the living room listening to adults talk...until Grandma and Grandpa got a television.

I don't think I ever spent time alone with Grandma until I was in high school. It was when Grandpa was hospitalized and we granddaughters were each assigned nights to stay with

Grandma. Grandma didn't need any special help and now I wonder if she really was uncomfortable being alone at night. It was an unsettling experience for me, anticipating spending long hours alone with an adult who was not my parent.

After school, instead of boarding my own school bus, I rode on the one that went out Main Street Road to her house. The first time, I worried about where I would sleep, what we would do, how I might respond if she talked about Grandpa's illness, and what I could say that would interest Grandma. Our routine was set the first day. I did homework and Grandma prepared supper. After doing dishes, we watched television or I did more homework until bedtime. Sometimes we talked. Or rather, Grandma listened. I became so comfortable that I even told her about my hopes and dreams.

Perhaps, it was Grandma's bedtime rituals that opened my heart. In her nightgown, each night she knelt at the side of her bed and prayed. Afterwards, sitting on the edge of the bed, she removed her thick elastic stockings, revealing ace bandages. When the bandages were unwound, I saw Grandma's bulging purple varicose veins. For the first time, I saw her vulnerability.

Less than five years later, in 1965, when I was only nineteen years old, I was the nurse who took care of Grandma Holscher the night she died. That night has reverberated through my whole life. I measure difficult experiences against that night. So far, it is still the most challenging.

Letter to Grandma Holscher

Dear Grandma,

How can I thank you for what you did for me on the night you died? I'm approaching seventy years and that night still remains the most challenging experience of my life. It could have turned out so differently without your willpower.

Grandma, I haven't told anyone this. When Aunt Loretta phoned me at nursing school and asked me to be your private duty nurse at the hospital. I could hear her desperation and I felt sorry for her. She had found a nurse for every shift except for the Saturday evening shift. When I said, "Yes," I didn't expect you to still be alive by Saturday.

I called home every day and learned that you were alert and talking with visitors, but still suffered from pain and nausea and weren't eating. I began to hope that you would die soon. I'm ashamed that I was so self-centered. Grandma, I'm sorry.

Is being only nineteen years old an excuse? I had never been with a dying person and didn't know that it was a privilege back then. If one of my patients had died in my hospital-based school, it would have been from a mistake or poor care on my part.

Saturday afternoon, when I walked down that long hospital corridor to your room, I felt so alone and was filled with dread. I prayed, "Dear God, don't let Grandma die on my shift." I wasn't ready to take care of any dying person without a teacher or mentor nearby! I'm sorry that I wasn't worrying about your comfort; I was scared that I wouldn't know how to take good enough care of you.

When I walked into your room, I entered the nightmare I had feared. All of your eight children were squeezed in your room...and their spouses...and your brother and your sister. I felt like you and I were on a stage. I worried about how I would be able to maintain and protect your dignity. I wasn't sure about what a good nurse would do for you in that situation.

The night wore on so slowly. There was so little that I could do for you. Turning you every couple of hours, some ice chips, placing a basin when your nausea turned to vomiting, and pain medications were all I could think to do.

A half hour before the end of my shift, Mrs. Thorne, your night nurse, stood in the doorway and looked at you. She caught my eye and said, "You've done a good job here. Come give me report and I'll take over. You can go home early." A sense a relief washed over me.

After reporting to Mrs. Thorne, I went back into your room to say goodbye. You were propped on your side and I did something completely out of character for our family. I bent down and kissed your cheek, like I do when I tuck a child into bed. You lifted your arm and we hugged and kissed and told each other, "Good-bye. I love you."

While I was driving home, I told myself that I had been a good enough nurse. You hadn't died during my shift. When I walked in the house fifteen minutes later, Mom was talking to someone on the phone. Imagine my surprise when she hung up the phone and told me that Dad had called to tell us that you had died! Only a few minutes earlier, you and I had been hugging.

Grandma, there is this movie called Groundhog Day where the main character keeps reliving the same day trying to get it right. I feel like I keep reliving the night you died. Will I ever truly understand what happened?

About ten years after you died, I read about an elderly Native American woman who called her family together for a potlatch because she was going to die. In a flash of insight, I realized that some people know they are about to die and, with a limited range of time, can choose the moment of their death.

I finally recognized the gift you had given me. Grandma, how could I have thought that my nursing care had kept you alive? You had stayed alive, even though you were nauseated and in pain, to protect me. Did you know that I probably couldn't have finished my nursing training if you had died on my watch? If only I had understood and appreciated your last heroic act of love at the time. I would never have chosen for you to suffer for my sake. I don't know how to thank you.

I'm a slow learner, Grandma. It was another twenty years before I had the next insight. In reliving that night, I realized that I hadn't seen any of the people in that hospital room hug, kiss or touch you lovingly. I know they loved and treasured you—it just wasn't our family's way of showing love. In fact, I don't think that you had hugged or kissed me since I was a toddler. I hadn't learned to give hugs freely yet. I wonder what the others in the room thought of my impulsive act? How did you have the strength to reach out to me like you did when your death was only minutes away? I hope at the end of my life, my last act will be one of love like yours.

I wonder how different my life would have been if Mrs. Thorne had said, "You've done a good job here. Come and give me report. Then, come back in and stay with your Grandma.

She's going to die soon. It's an honor to be with someone at their death. I'll teach you how to be present with a dying person. This will be a memory that you will treasure."

Forty years after you died, Grandma, I offered that invitation to my niece and your great-granddaughter Megan when Mom was dying.

Twenty-three year-old Megan had been sitting with me in Mom's room. When we were called for supper, Megan stepped out of the room and fell into my arms, sobbing, "Why does death have to be so ugly?"

Instead of eating supper, Megan and I sat outside on the old swing set and I told her about your waiting for me to leave before dying. Then, I felt a nudge to tell more stories to help Megan see death differently. Were you prodding me, Grandma?

With each story, I wondered whether the stories could free Megan from the fear of being with dying people—the fear that that I had for years after your death.

While I was telling Megan stories, Mom had a visit from her long-dead brother Henry. Mom told those sitting with her, "Henry came for me. I told him that I wasn't quite ready, but that I'd be ready soon. I need a little more time before I go." Did Mom, like you, need to take care of a granddaughter?

Grandma, do you know if Mom was surprised when Megan came back the next morning with her mother?

Mom laughed with Megan, my sisters and me when we watched the videotape recorded the night before of three-year-old Carson blowing out his birthday candles over and over again.

When Mom settled into a deep sleep, Megan sat at the bedside with us girls. Mom began having the noisy irregular breathing like the kind that often occurs before a death. We all sat quietly and breathed in unison with Mom. Eventually, there were long pauses in her breathing, during which Mom's face became smooth and as serene as a painting of the Madonna.

I signaled Megan to sit beside me, whispering to her, "Watch Mom's face."

Megan saw it, too. When Mom's breathing paused, Megan whispered in awe, "Her wrinkles are gone!"

I smiled and responded, "Her face is as smooth as a newborn baby napping, isn't it?"

Mom's breathing was the only sound in her room, until Mary Ellen opened the door and asked, "What's happening here?"

We signaled for quiet, just like we would do when a baby is napping and we don't want it to wake up. But Mary Ellen persisted, "Don't you recognize snoring when you hear it? Mom's just snoring."

As if on cue, Mom's breathing became quiet and regular. She continued to sleep soundly. We all scattered, thinking that Mom probably would die with the setting sun.

Megan and Mary Ellen stayed in the room and were the only ones at Mom's bedside when she quietly slipped away. I'd like to think that you were watching over them, Grandma.

After Mom died, I hope you heard Megan telling me, "Aunt Janie, I was present, just sitting on the chair, not touching Grandma, but breathing with her and thinking about what a good Grandma she was. Aunt Mary Ellen was holding her hand. It was meant to be that we were the only ones in the room, because Grandma, Aunt Mary Ellen and I all have the same initials -- MEH."

A few minutes after Mom died, Mary Ellen told me, "I couldn't have lived with myself if I hadn't been holding Mom's hand when she died."

I want to believe that Mom told Uncle Henry she wasn't quite ready to go, because she wanted to have that special time with Megan and Mary Ellen.

Grandma, I felt so grateful when I overheard Megan at the funeral home telling her Great Aunts (your daughters) about Mom's death. She described Mom's wrinkles disappearing and how Mom looked like as precious as a newborn baby sleeping. Megan actually used the word "beautiful" to describe Mom's dying. Can I dare to hope that she won't be afraid the next time she's with someone who's dying?

All my life, I have measured challenges against how I felt walking down the hospital hallway to your room, Grandma. If I had had a little more wisdom and stayed after my shift was over, would I be holding the night that you died as one of the most precious incidents of my life, like Megan does Mom's death?

When I recall your death, Grandma, the meaning of your last night has changed time and again. At first, I thought it was about my being a good enough nurse. Then I came to understand that you loved me enough to suffer for hours to protect me. After that, I realized that I had given you a gift by returning to your room, not as your nurse, but as your granddaughter hugging and kissing you before I went home. Eventually, I realized that, with the right person at my side, I could have had a totally different experience.

Your death was like a rainbow; how I saw it depended on where I stood. With time and a broadened life experience, I review that night from other viewpoints and new insights have surfaced. Your gift, Grandma, has become richer as I age.

I thank you, Grandma, for being such a positive force in my life. We weren't close in the storybook way of grandparents and grandchildren. I was only one of dozens of grandchildren. Yet, in one significant moment, you shaped my future.

I love you.

Janie

Uncle Maurice and Uncle Merle

Maurice and Merle were the names on the polished surface of two tombstones each etched with a little lamb.

Mom and Dad, as well as my uncles and aunts, called them "poor babies" when we placed flowers at their grave sites each Memorial Day. No one told me their story about them.

A yellowed newspaper clipping said that they died of scarlet fever.

When I interviewed my father's oldest brother Uncle Willy about the event, the implications of the difficult year of 1921 began to take shape.

Their story slowly unfolded as I matured.

Before I could read, I thought that Maurice and Merle died the day they were born, like my baby cousin. I thought the lamb on each of their tombstones meant they died in their infancy.

When I could do simple arithmetic, I realized that they were three and four years old when they died and I began to picture them as Dad's toddler-age brothers. I must have been approaching my teens before I understood that they were born before my Dad. They were Grandma and Grandpa's third and fourth children.

When Grandma was pregnant with Dad, the family was stricken with scarlet fever. Grandma did not become ill herself and neither did the baby, my Aunt Ruth. Because the family was quarantined, Grandma had to single-handedly nurse my grandfather and the four boys who were ill while also maintaining the household. Neighbors could only bring food to the doorstep and wish them well through the closed window. I don't know if they had any medicines or medical advice. Grandma managed to feed and tend the ill, as well as take care of the baby Ruth, while keeping the stove burning, etc.

Both the little boys died on the same day. Grandma dressed them in the best clothes and laid them on the couch with their feet touching. She had to watch the undertaker put the bodies of three-year-old Maurice and four-year-old Merle in tiny caskets. Then, she must have watched him take the children in for Grandpa to see them one last time.

Because of the quarantine and my grandfather's guarded condition, Grandma knew that there would be no wake and no one in their home could attend the boys' funeral.

When I was studying to be a nurse and learned about scarlet fever, I realized that I might have known Uncle Maurice and Uncle Merle as men older than my father, if their illness had happened after antibiotics had been developed.

When Lisa and Lynda were babies and both in diapers, I speculated about how exhausted Grandma must have been and how utterly alone she must have felt with all of the work that she had to manage all by herself.

As a hospice nurse, I wondered if she and Grandpa had a chance to truly grieve the boys' passing as she continued to care for Grandpa. Less than six months after Maurice and Merle's deaths, my father was born. Grandma surely was still grieving the loss of her young sons. Now as a widow, I suspect that her grief must have dampened her ability to love my father.

I wonder what new insights I will have about this event in the future.

FAMILY STORIES

I've always thought that
a big laugh is
a really loud noise from the soul saying,
"Ain't that the truth."

Quincy Jones

What Did He Say?

No photograph could convey an incident that occurred midway on our four-day horsepacking trip in Yosemite's high country. While the guides were assigning each of us a mule, I anticipated splendid scenery, breathtaking sunsets and good company. I was confident that my ten rolls of film would document the beauty of the High Sierras.

Within the first hour, we learned that the Curry Company choses its mules for their ability to follow the rear end in front of them rather than for having a gait like a rocking chair. We soon found out that the mules' names fit their characters or characteristics. My husband Jim's mule was named Gunsmoke. She was powdery gray and was a female with a mind of her own.

One day, we were working our way through a series of switchbacks down a mountain with a river of water gliding down its side only twenty feet to our right. Gunsmoke lost sight of the ass in front of her and began sniffing some mule droppings that had been deposited on the trail days before. Despite Jim's efforts to pull her head up and get her to move along, she kept her nose to the ground checking out the maggots in the "biscuits" at her feet.

I was behind Jim and could see that our guide Bill, who was already at the bottom of the switchbacks, had turned around and was eyeing the half of his party stalled behind the recalcitrant Gunsmoke. Bill was no spring chicken and had seen it all on the trail. Maybe it was from all those years as a cowboy, or maybe cowboys just don't talk much, but we found Bill to be a man who chose his words carefully and used them sparingly.

Bill raised his hand to his mouth and shouted up instructions to Jim. Above the sound of the rushing water, two words came up the mountainside. "Feed her," Bill called.

Turning around to me, Jim repeated with a puzzled look on his face, "Feed her?" I replied, "Yep, that's what it sounds like to me." Jim looked around for something to give Gunsmoke. All either of us could see were the tough three to four feet high manzanita shrubs squeezing either side of the trail. Certainly, no grass could possibly be growing under its thick cover. Did Bill mean for Jim to give Gunsmoke the apple in his lunch bag?

Again Bill called up. This time we agreed that we both heard Bill say, "Beat her!" Jim's eyes searched for a stick or branch, while kicking Gunsmoke's sides with no effect.

Just as Jim began to dismount to find something on the ground to use to get Gunsmoke's attention, Bill's two words floated up again. "Lead her," he called.

Jim hesitated, wondering if the gentle breeze, the cascading waters or the impaired hearing of the middle-aged could be garbling Bill's advice once more.

Uncertainly, Jim dismounted, grabbed the reins and jerked Gunsmoke's head around and led the way down to the rest of the party waiting below.

Gunsmoke followed willingly. She had an ass to follow.

Our Star

Jim didn't suspect that he would be placing that star on the top of our family's Christmas trees for nearly thirty years when he made the gold star to top our first Christmas tree

We were struggling newlyweds thousands of miles away from our hometown at the time. When I looked at the five-foot tree in our living room, images of my family's past Christmas trees surfaced. Each year, my mother and my brothers and sisters and I had burrowed through the boxes searching for our favorite ornaments. If you carefully untangled the gleeful voices, you could have heard, "Remember when I got this ornament?" "This has always been my favorite." "We got this when Henry was fascinated with cowboys." Lovingly worn ornaments recalled a treasured moment in one of our lives. After all the ornaments were in place, my mother and selected siblings added the final touch of tinsel, placed in single strands perpendicular to the floor.

Jim's voice brought me back to our apartment. "How are we going to decorate this tree?" I interpreted his statement to mean, "How can we manage buying any decorations?"

My younger brothers and sisters unintentionally provided the solution. They had pooled their resources and sent us an early Christmas present—a Nativity Set, cookie cutters and a cookie sheet. The note with the gifts reminded me of the weekend three years earlier when I had purchased cookie cutters myself and started a tradition of baking and decorating cookies with them. They wanted to be sure that I could continue that tradition in my new home. The following day, I purchased the ingredients to make sugar cookies. Instead of being eaten, these cookies would ornament our tree. Even when we added the silver strands of tinsel, the tree didn't look complete. We tucked the Nativity set under the tree. Still, it looked unfinished.

Jim thought that the tree needed something on the top. He playfully designed a star from the gold foil box that had held the long stem red roses he had given me for my birthday just a few weeks before. Being an engineer, he made the star's pattern by combining two equilateral triangles, making a perfect six-pointed star. A paper clip taped to the back of the star held it to the tree's top. Jim felt that the gold star was the perfect finishing touch. When that Christmas season was over, I saved his star with the nativity set.

Jim was surprised, and somewhat dismayed, when I asked him to put the star on top of the Christmas tree the following year. The third year, Jim offered to go shopping with me and help me find a better topper. Nothing we found pleased us both, so the star topped our tree year after year.

As our children grew older and helped decorate our Christmas tree, they searched for the star in our growing assortment of the Christmas ornaments. They would gaily set it aside for Jim. His placing the star on the top of the tree became a family ritual, signaling that tree decorating was complete. Eventually, they noticed and enjoyed Jim's chagrin as he put the star in its place. Sometimes, I think he grumbled and bemoaned the placement of the star to feed the kids' reaction to his discomfort.

Jim was relieved of his star placement duties by our friend Cathie. That change was connected to my birthday—my 50th. At the first Christmas Tree Lane, a fund raiser that culminated in the drawing of winning tickets for sumptuously decorated trees, Cathie won a tree festooned with golden angels and red ribbons. Her husband Harlan's parting words that day echoed in her mind, "Have fun, but don't bring one of those trees home. We don't have room for another one here." Cathie was torn between a desire to respect Harlan's request and wanting to enjoy the tree. Then, she remembered that the event was held on my birthday, and she impulsively decided to give me the tree. That evening when the tree was delivered, Cathie, Harlan, Jim and I were celebrating my birthday together. Harlan audibly sighed when the fully decorated tree was delivered. Jim sighed, too, and said, "This year, I finally get to retire that poor old cardboard star," pointing to a stunning golden angel on top of the tree. I also sighed because I thought that our tradition of thirty years had finally run its course.

The following year, I permanently retired the star. Jim had died of cancer two months earlier and the star stayed in the box with the ornaments.

Two years later, our oldest daughter, Lisa, asked for the star. Alyssa, her first child and our first grandchild, had been born in July and she wanted the star to grace the top of their Christmas tree.

While I searched for the star in the boxes of ornaments, I recalled the sense of playfulness that characterized our Christmases. I delighted in the feelings of family solidarity that reached all the way back to my home in Indiana. I thought about how the commonplace can be elevated by love and tradition.

Clothes Make the Man

"You aren't from here, are you?" The woman smiled softly and looked up at my father. Then her eyes moved toward the two empty chairs facing her across the table. She waved her arm toward the seats and added, "We would be glad to have you join us."

Dad put his tray on the table. As he sat down, he asked, "How did you know we aren't from here?"

Dad was so used to wearing overalls, he didn't realize that they made him standout in most crowds. When I had invited Mom and Dad to join Jim and me on a trip to Washington, DC, I had told them that they could wear whatever was comfortable, knowing that I was giving Dad permission to wear his Oshkosh B'Gosh bib overalls. I certainly wouldn't have made that offer when I was a teenager, or even while I was in my 20s. It took living through the teen years of our three children to soften me up. This trip, his overalls were still a deep blue, washed only enough to make them comfortably soft.

Dad was nearly seventy years old. His hair had hardly changed over the years, although it had thinned a little and was graying at the edges. The 5'8" height of his youth was just starting to shrink. His clothing concealed his bowed legs and huge chest. That woman couldn't have guessed the strength of his well-worn muscles or steely will. She wouldn't have a chance to call up his extensive databank of weather conditions, events, crops and horses, with associated dates, locations and people. She, like most people, would remember his unwavering pale sky-blue eyes.

The restaurant near the Library of Congress was crowded with people dressed in casual clothing that warm spring Saturday morning. Described as a "favorite breakfast place among locals" by the guidebook, the small establishment was a cross between a fast food place and a coffee house. The dark wood-paneled walls contrasted with the white formica table tops and bright primary blue chairs and table legs. Sun streamed into the room from the spotless front windows. A few people were reading, but most of the patrons were talking animatedly with others at their tables. When we entered, there was not one empty table in the place!

What a way to start the day, I grumbled to myself. *I wanted this first trip to DC to be special for Mom and Dad. How could I know that this place would be overflowing, even on a Saturday? Now that we all have our food and coffee, where are we going to sit to eat it?*

My stomach growled, not from hunger, but anxiety. I looked around the restaurant and felt my spine shrinking, not from age like Dad's, but pressed down by disappointment.

The man at the cash register must have read my body language. He said, "People are used to sharing tables with strangers here. There are plenty of empty chairs. Just ask if they mind if you join them.

Slowly, I turned to face Mom, Dad and my husband Jim.

"We are going to have to split up," I said. Letting my eyes wander around the room, I continued, "I see several tables with two seats. What about Mom and me sitting together? Dad and Jim, would you be okay without us?"

That is how Dad and Jim met the black-haired charming woman from Peru who worked at the Library of Congress. Almost as soon as they sat down with her and her friend, they joined the ranks of the animated conversationalists. In fact, the four of them continued chatting long after their food and coffee had been consumed.

Mom and I stood to leave the restaurant. Dad and Jim kept talking to the two women.

Mom and I walked past their table as we left the restaurant. The conversation continued. I doubt if they even noticed us.

Mom and I stood outside the window where they were sitting. Our men still didn't notice us.

I almost tapped the window to get their attention, but decided to go back into the restaurant to get them.

Once all four of us were together outside Dad said, "That gal knew we weren't from here."

With a smile that began on his lips, creased his cheeks and sparked in his gray-blue eyes, Jim put his hand on Dad's shoulder and said, "Didn't you know that was just a line. She was trying to pick you up!"

Dad's chest got bigger and he looked taller. A crooked smile materialized and his eyes twinkled. He closed his right hand around the buckle of the right overalls strap.

Little did we know that, within the hour, those overalls would be the center of attention at the Capitol Building.

Always Prepared

"Now, who in this line would need that sign?" Jim pointed to sign posted above a three-foot high metal can. "No weapons allowed in Capitol Building. Place all guns and knives here."

Mom laughed. "Dad, you better check your overalls for weapons."

I was relieved that everyone was still in a good mood.

We had been standing in line waiting to get into the Capitol Building on a warm Saturday morning in April of 1992 for a half hour. Before entering the building we would be going through metal detectors that had been installed after the assassination attempt on Reagan.

Upon entering the building, we were assigned to three different lines. We each put our coins and other metal items in bowls. My line moved the quickest, so I found a place where I could easily be seen by the others. Mom and Jim soon joined me. We all watched and waited for Dad to go through his metal detector.

"BR-R-R-R," a detector blared.

I scrutinized each person in a detector, looking for a rough-and-tough-looking fellow. *Is one of them a potential assassin? Where should I run if there is trouble? Dad's right up there with the "bad one." Dad! He's the one setting off the alarm! What are they going to do to him?*

Everyone else's eyes turned toward that line, too.

We all watched my dad slowly reach into the long narrow pocket on his right leg and pull out a pair of pliers. He handed them to the frowning man in uniform.

They sent Dad through the detector again.

"GR-R-R-R," it blared again. The security men stood straighter and stiffer, eying my dad. People shuffled nervously and looked for safe hiding places. I edged along the metal fence to the security area, getting as close as I could to my father.

My dad reached into the longer pocket on the same leg. This time he retrieved a screwdriver.

As he handed it to the guard, I heard him say, "Maybe this is the problem."

Behind me, Jim muttered, "Why does he have those with him? Did he think the Capitol was going to need repairs?"

Dad went through the device again.

"RR-R-R-R."

Dad said, "Please, guys, don't make me take my overalls off. It has to be these metal buckles. There are ladies here and we'd all be embarrassed."

The two guards exchanged glances.

"Do you have any weapons in any of those pockets?" one of them asked.

Dad shook his head, "No."

The one holding the tools handed them to Dad. He took them and retrieved his coins and wallet. Hands full, he walked over to us.

We were all shaken by our first brush with metal detectors and tight security.

Dad carefully put his tools back in his pockets. Safe from marauders, we began our tour of the Capitol Building.

As we walked along a corridor, Jim asked Dad, "What did you plan to do with those tools? Did you think a hinge might have a loose screw or something?"

Dad replied, "You never know when they will come in handy." He patted each of his pockets and named the contents. "Pencil. Notepad. Pocket watch. Coins. Wallet. Handkerchief. Screwdriver. Pliers. Pocketknife."

"What?" Jim hissed. "Didn't you see the sign about the knives?"

"I've carried it for twenty years. It isn't a weapon." Dad reached in his pocket to show it to Jim.

"Leave it where it is. You could get us all put in jail."

When we left the building, we passed by the still-empty metal container. Now we knew what kind of people should heed that sign.

MESSENGERS

Animals are supremely spiritual beings in their own right. We as humans have long overlooked this and have often thought of them somehow inferior to us in all ways. When we are able to make the connection that animals are part of us and part of the greater cosmic fabric that makes up our lives, then we can truly begin to learn more about the world around us, the world within us, and the spiritual nature of the cosmos.

Ted Andrews

Bird Messengers

Jim died in a hospital in Austin. All three of our children were there, as well as the Dave and Chris. He died just as the sun was rising.

Lisa, Dave, Lynda, Chris and Dan had been sleeping in the waiting room and slipping into his room for a few minutes at a time throughout the night. About a half-hour before Jim died, they all came into in his room, as if they had been alerted. They all found a place by his bed, almost circling him and they placed their hands on him. Jim took one last dramatic breath, almost sitting upright, and then he was gone. We stayed with Jim's body for an hour or so. Then we went back to Lisa and Dave's home.

I sat numbly at their kitchen table just staring out the window while Lisa made breakfast. At some point, two doves caught my eye. They were perched together on the fence to the right of the window. The two birds sat side by side with their heads turned to each other, as if they were engaged in an intense conversation.

When we all sat down to breakfast, I wanted to show the doves to the kids, but they were nowhere to be seen. However, under the bird feeder, a single adult dove and five small doves busily pecked the birdseed droppings from the bird feeder. I turned my attention to my kids at the table and realized that we were sitting around the table in the same configuration as the birds outside.

Maybe that made me sensitive to the birds who reached out to me a few days later. We were finally driving back to California after dealing with lots of red tape in order to cremate Jim. Jim's ashes were still warm when we picked him up at the crematorium the afternoon we finally left Texas to return home.

Lynda, Dan and I had decided to drive back to California non-stop. That night, I fell asleep with Jim's ashes next to me.

When I awakened, I thought that I was still in a dream. The car shuttered as if a giant was lightly tapping us with its finger. I saw Lynda and Dan in the front seat, but I couldn't see beyond the beige fog outside the windows.

"What's happening?" I asked sleepily.

"We're in a sand storm," Dan responded.

Lynda clarified, "Hardly anyone is on the road. I've been watching the lines on the side of the road to help Dan. We haven't been able to see anything beyond the road for hours."

I stretched, and then leaned forward placing my hand on the front seat to the right of Dan's shoulder. "You two must really be tired. Why don't you let me drive for a while?"

Dan replied. "We're getting low on gas. We can trade at the next gas station."

I sat back and peered out the window. Were those images out there or was the sand thicker in places? The sound of the wind was muffled by the car's motor. It felt like our car had been transformed into a tiny airplane flying through clouds of ashes and buffeted by whirling air currents.

The monotony dulled my senses. My eyelids drooped and I drifted into sleep until the sound of the car's wheels on rough pavement nudged me into wakefulness. I saw a strip of buildings on either side of the road. I noticed a billboard with a line of birds sitting atop it and a gas station ahead on the right.

As Dan turned off, the birds on the billboard rose as one wheeling around in the sky overhead performing a perfectly timed ballet of swoops and swirls with their wings whisper close, but never touching. When Dan stopped, they settled back onto the billboard.

When I stepped out to fill the gas tank, I heard the birds chattering. Holding the nozzle in place, I tried to see them. Just then I noticed that a group of pigeons had taken the stage, performing their own acrobatic choreography, as the other birds chattered nearby. A bit of sunlight reflected from the white of their outstretched wings and sparkled. The metal roof above me and the top of the billboard across the street framed their acrobatic flights of fancy.

Another sound pecked at me. A soft "Whoo wh-o-o," purred repeatedly from some place above and behind me. My eyes roved the area. Finally, they settled on a brownish shape in the corner of the overhang. "Whoo wh-o-o," I heard again from that odd shape. Two eyes looked directly into mine and I knew it was an owl. Once I saw it, it stopped calling.

An owl in daylight. In the roof over a gas station. I know that it did not belong there, any more than those birds should have been dancing.

I would like to think Jim was letting me know he was nearby. I can't be sure, but I want it to be so.

This was my introduction to animals as messengers. When animals behave in uncharacteristic ways, I try to figure out whether I'm being given a message. It's rarely as clear as these incidents.

13 Snakes

The spring of 13 snakes
    where I had never
        seen a snake before
          and haven't
        seen one
        since.
    The spring of 13 snakes
gopher snakes
rattlesnakes
  gartersnakes
    alive snakes
      dead snakes
        wood snake
        snakes on paths
          in grass
            on road
        in hawk's beak
      remind me
    Free yourself
Shed old ways
Grow
  Change
    Trust
      Be true
        to the inner
          you.

Hawk Sighting

Those of us who saw the hawk didn't talk about them until after Mom's funeral. How I wish I could have seen the dance that Mark and Carson saw!

A hawk sat on horse pasture fence veiled by morning fog in
        pink dawn. I was sitting at Mom's bedside in
        sunroom. It was the morning of the day that Mom
        died.

A hawk sitting on fence post beside road in early morning fog.
        Mark in his pickup passes it and hawk flies to next
        fence post. Pickup passes it again and hawk flies to
        next fence post. *Strange behavior*, Mark thought. *It's a*
        hawk, isn't it? Pickup passes hawk and it flies away.
        It was the morning of the day that Mom died.

Hawk on tree top across the road from St. Vincent's Cemetery. It
        was the day of Mom's burial. Lori saw it. So, did I.

Two hawks soar and swoop up and down almost wingtip to
        wingtip. Mark and Carson saw it the afternoon of
        Mom's funeral and burial. They watched the two
        hawks for several minutes.

Hawk

On the day that our mother died
    I saw you
        blurred by the pink dawn fog.
    You were on fencepost
        watching Mom sleep?

On the day that our mother died
    Mark saw you
    Each time he drove by
        You flew to next post
        "I see you," said Mark.
    Then you flew away.

On the day that our mother was buried
    We saw you
        On the top of the tallest pine
        Watching us bid Mom good-bye

On the afternoon that our mother was buried
    They saw you
    Reunited
    Soaring and swooping
    Wingtip to wingtip

Did Mom finally get Dad to dance?

WEATHER

Weather forecast for tonight: dark.

George Carlin

In my birth family, weather is a part of conversations.
So, being true to my roots, let's talk weather…..

Cold, Cold, Cold

When I recall the trip to Yosemite on the Labor Day weekend of 2000, cold fingers creep up my spine.

The night before our horsepacking trip, we stayed in one of the Tuolumne Meadows tent cabins. Even with a long sleeved top, a sweatsuit, socks and a double comforter, I was cold.

I dreamed cold dreams, uncivilized dreams. Snow suddenly appeared in summer. Trips on horses went bad. Other riders and horses slid off scary, narrow trails. Bears wondered through campgrounds, rattling tents. All of my dreams were unsettling, most were cold.

The next morning, like the sun burning off the fog, the warm shower and hot breakfast lifted the lingering hangover from the previous night's dreams.

At the stable, my son Dan and I met our guides Christy and Dinah. Christy looked like a Barbie doll in jeans and fitted denim jacket. At the nape of her neck, neatly tied long blonde hair hung, like a horse's tail, nearly to her waist. The ten-gallon hat on her head seemed oversized. Dinah, on the other hand, looked more seasoned. Her skin was leathery. A practical tired-looking Stetson hat covered shoulder-length, dull, palomino colored hair. She wore leather chaps and a long canvas duster.

There were only two other people on this trip, Ken and Michelle McCarty. Dan and I ogled as they pulled bag after bag from their car. Dan looked at me with pointed eyebrows, "Did they read the same brochure that you sent me?"

We waited to see our guides' reaction. "Take all you want," said Christy. "You are the only ones on this trip and we have two pack mules."

While Christy and Dinah balanced our belongings on the mules, big fluffy snowflakes drifted down. Christy looked up at the sky, grinned from ear to ear, "I never thought I would see this. This is too-oo good."

Dan and I were almost infected by her enthusiasm at the passing snow flurry. But a nagging concern prompted me to retrieve my raincoat from my duffle bag. I imagined a scenario where the snow turned to rain. I thought that the raincoat would offer more protection than the poncho I had put in my saddlebag. Thinking about the scenic high country, I stuffed my camera into my coat pocket to get some memorable shots of the mountains. I mounted Cadillac the mule assigned to me feeling prepared for our adventure.

Christy led us out of the stable area. She turned around, still smiling, and waved her right arm skyward, saying, "Isn't this great? We are so lucky to get to see snow at this time of the year."

Within a half hour, we began to fear that this was not a passing snow flurry. The vistas and distant landmarks that I had anticipated seeing again were obscured by the hovering bleak clouds. The snow was accompanied by a cold, biting wind.

The trip, which should have been filled with scenic wonders, became a day-long test of our endurance. The awkward safety helmet became an object of comfort, keeping my head warm. Christy rode at the front and I could see her tucking her neck down between her shoulders, letting go of the reins and pulling her hands into the sleeves of the slicker she had donned over her jacket. She had a scarf over her nose and mouth.

Several times, Christy turned around and reassured us, "My horse knows this trail. He can find it even when I can't see it."

I worried, *Is Christy saying that she can't see the trail herself? Is she trusting her horse to lead us to Sunrise Camp because she can't orient herself? Does she depend on major landmarks, peaks and distant objects, which are obscured now, to find our trail?* A change in the quality of the snow distracted me from these disturbing thoughts.

I thought of the numerous words the Russian language has for snow and wondered how many of them I could use this day. I wished I could list the kinds of snow I saw in succinct English words. At times the snowflakes were huge, puffy, light and nearly one inch across, gently drifting down. Those were the kind that tempted me to tilt my face up to the sky and stick out my tongue, just to feel the soft touch of the cool snow and experience its sizzle when it melted on my tongue. Those flakes were silhouetted against the dark pines and cedars, slowly falling to their resting place. Our surroundings were unusually quiet. The noises were limited to the clomp and ring of our mules hooves against the dirt and rocks. The snow wrapped us in its muffler.

At the other extreme, hard, tiny pellets were hurled into our bodies by frigid, clawing wind. I could hear them ping as they struck my helmet and crackle against my coat. Those compacted bits of ice made my hands even feel colder and I swaddled myself more securely in my coat. I constantly checked my hood to make sure the wind hadn't shoved it off my helmet.

I began to respond to the cold, as if it were a roaring, hot fire. When a part of my body became too cold, I moved to protect it, while exposing another part. I shifted the reins from hand to hand, keeping one hand in my coat pocket to warm it. Just as often, I had to rearrange my coat to cover a knee. I noticed that my coat seemed to be pulled forward on the side with the hand in the pocket, exposing the knee on the side of my uncovered hand. I was freezing myself one side at a time.

Snow swirled, drifted, and pelleted. Sometimes, it was accompanied by piercing wind, breezes, or no wind at all. The sun rarely peeked through, leaving us in a blurry world, surrounded by snowflakes and veils of foggy moisture. I became thankful when we could see our guides front and back and into the trees on either side.

Tales of survival in dire circumstances haunted me. I thought of the characters in Shackleton's *Endurance*, Rawicz's *The Long Walk*, and Wallis's *Two Old Women*. How would I respond to those conditions?

I reminded myself, *You know how resilient the human body is! Why are you fantasizing like this?*

My reverie was interrupted by Christy's joking with Dan, "We are just like the Donner party!"

Maybe I should have reviewed those sagas for survival tips, I thought.

Long before our stop at noon, we all were very aware of not being dressed for the weather. We eyed the Gore-Tex gloves Dan was wearing with envy.

Christy waved a gloved hand and said, "I have two pairs of wool gloves. This pair is already wet, but I'm saving my dry ones for the second half of the ride."

Dinah said, "A wet glove is much better than no glove. I speak from experience. I have tried it both ways on this ride."

As mentioned earlier, I didn't have any gloves and rode one handed and put the other in my pocket. Dan looked at my ruby red hand. He said, "Are you doing okay?"

I nodded my head and smiled. "My hands are only cold. There are no signs of frostbite."

When we reached Cathedral Lakes, another group was already at the site. Christy dismounted and tied her horse and she said, "Wait for me to hold your mule, while you dismount."

She started with Ken, leading his mule to an upright two-foot log. She held the rope and reached up to place her hands against his left hip, but he didn't move. With a rumbling panic in her voice, she called out to one of the young male guides of the other group, "Can you help me?"

Together, they supported Ken. Slowly, his right leg came out of the stirrup and with their verbal encouragement, he gradually moved the leg over the mule's back. Together, they eased him to the ground.

Next, they came to me. I worried that I, too, would be frozen in my saddle. Despite my concern, my legs moved. I swung my right leg over the saddle, lifted myself and felt my right foot touch the ground. Almost instinctively, I put both hands nearer my body's warmth in my jeans pockets.

Christy and Dan devised an elaborate glove swap. Dan, being the gallant person he was, gave me his gloves. Christy gave him her wet pair and she changed into her dry pair. Ah, the warmth of gloved hands.

Another horsepacking group was also there and we got acquainted, while we ate our lunches.

Looking up the trail which they had descended a few minutes earlier, a gray-bearded man told us, "We spent last night at Sunrise Camp. It was cold up there and they were out of firewood! I'm glad to be returning to civilization." Again, I pictured myself living in the survival tales I had recently read.

Lunch was a shivery affair. I held my food in gloved hands, taking the gloves off only to open a package. We all swayed, stomped and moved about to keep our limbs warm and get our blood circulating. No one even looked for a dry spot to sit down to eat.

Cathedral Lakes' character had changed with the storm. It wasn't the inviting clear blue mirror reflecting a cloudless sky and surrounding peaks that I remembered from a prior trip. Instead, it was only a small, dark gray, cold spot surrounded by snow. The inhospitable feeling was heightened by wind racing down the meadow. It grabbed our clothes, whipping off our hoods and loosening our carefully positioned outer garments.

As we were mounting our mules again, a mule train passed by the lake. The two guides were each leading five mules. Christy explained, "They are bringing garbage down from Sunrise." She waved a greeting to them and told us, "I'm going to talk to them about the trail conditions."

She returned smiling. "They told me that they just delivered food and firewood to Sunrise."

With raised hopes, we mounted our steeds.

The clouds lifted and the sun shined on us. Soothing warmth penetrated to our cores. I searched for a horizon or an expansive view. The surrounding mist and shortened views made the sunlight seem like an aberration. We were entwined by a muffled white-shrouded, surreal world. As if teasing us, the sun slid back into the gray, swirling clouds. The toasty calm was replaced by chilling winds, which tossed snowflakes at us. The storm seemed colder for the brief respite.

As we crossed one of the meadows, a running figure passed us on the left. He wore a backpack and his heals seemed to be pulled out of his sneakers with each step into ankle deep snow. Like a modern day Mad Hatter, he called out, "I'm late. I'm late for work."

As he disappeared into the misty curtains, I thought, *I wonder what he does. Could he work at our camp? I hope he isn't the cook! I would hate to have a cold supper after this!*

We approached our destination, Sunrise High Sierra Camp at 2:00 p.m.

Was this the same camp we had visited in 1990? Where would the manager have been sitting? That day, we had all envied her "corporate office," a 2½ by 3 foot wooden table sitting on the rocks above overlooking the meadow. Her golden red hair was bathed in the gentle sunlight. The campground seemed to be poised behind her on a shelf sheltered by a wall of biscuit-like rocks piled upon one another, rising to make Sunrise Peak.

Christy pointed through the falling snow to our right and called back, "See those white tents? You will be staying in one of those tonight." Their pointed tops could barely be distinguished.

When I dismounted at the area where the animals were kept, my legs felt strangely stiff and uncoordinated. I was also somewhat disoriented since the tents that Christy had pointed out on our approach were no longer visible.

After we had all dismounted, Christy pointed, "That trail goes to the camp. Go to the office and get your tent assignments. Dinah and I will bring your bags up there for you."

Dan and I were in front and couldn't see any distinctive trail or any of the tents. I said, "Could that black line in the snow be the trail?"

We followed it to a dead end, where I clumsily stepped into a tiny stream.

We four tourists conferred found another likely line and, following it, found a few tents. Wondering around, we found a tent with a sign "Store Closed" hanging by the door.

Dan tried the door anyway and it opened. We shuffled into the tent. The walls were a toasty yellow-brown, but it was dim inside. The word "cave" came to my mind. Our eyes were drawn towards people sitting on folding chairs huddled around an iron stove. We saw bright flames licking chopped wood through its open front door. When our eyes adjusted to the darkened room, we could see tables with chairs atop them where we would be eating our supper later in the evening. None of the people seemed to be the manager we were seeking. Wordlessly, the people around the fire began shifting and slowly rising to make room for us.

We gladly moved into the inner circle inches from the stove, stretching our hands to the light and warmth. Gradually, I became aware of the people as individuals, noticing that they were all fully dressed in outdoor clothing.

One of the men spoke up, "I bet you wonder why we are here? Firewood is rationed up here. We are gathered at this fire in order to have a few pieces of wood for a nighttime fire in our own tents."

"You would think we would at least get a decent fire for the price we paid," another man grumbled.

"We only have wool blankets on our beds here. It doesn't make sense. When we were at Merced Lake Camp, which is lower and warmer, we had comforters on the beds for warmth. I think we should have those here, too."

"We may not have comforters at this camp, but we do have million-dollar hot showers," a slim, middle-aged woman laughed. "I heard that the money was donated by a rich, dedicated backpacker to build an environmentally sensitive facility." Turning to us newcomers, she continued, "Wait until you see it! They say it costs a million dollars because everything was first rate and all the wood had to be brought in by mule."

Just then, the Mad Hatter appeared behind the counter of the "store" holding a clipboard. He too was dressed in snow clothes, but his curly reddish chin-length blonde hair was uncovered. "Hi. I'm Brian," he said. "I'm ready to give you your tent assignments."

Looking at Dan and me, he said, "You are in Tent 4." We stayed by the stove.

Christy and Dinah came in the store and said, "Your duffle bags are on a tarp to the left of the office."

As if choreographed, those clustered around the stove slid aside to open two chairs by the stove's door. Christy and Dinah sat in the inner circle and the group closed around them.

Brian looked at them and then his clipboard. He said, "Don't settle in to the equipment room yet. I think some people aren't going to show up today. Then, you two can have a tent." They looked at each other and grinned.

Finally warmed, Dan and I decided to find our tent. My heavy duffle bag had two inches of snow on it. Dan lifted it and helped me place its strap securely on my shoulder. Loaded like mules, we hunted for our cabin, using the paths and avoiding the puddles.

Tent 4 had a two-foot puddle in front of the rock that was our doorstep. Dan stepped up to the rock, leaned to the left and into the tent to open the screen door. I grabbed it and opened it against the right wall to step inside. Our housekeeping tent had a cement floor, two twin beds, a stove, a bucket with seven pieces of firewood, an equal number of kindling pieces wrapped in a single page of newspaper, a card table, two folding chairs, two open lockers, and a candle.

Unpacking my gear, I found that about half of my clothes had been dampened by the snow and began to hang them on the hooks around one side of the tent. Dan and I lined our wettest clothes on the wall behind the cold stove, hoping that they would drip damp that afternoon and fully dry out that night when we built our own fire.

Hungering for warmth again, I decided to use the million dollar bath facility to take a shower.

I had to walk up a dozen steps up to the door, but they didn't seem to be icy or be snow covered, like everything else. The facility was raised to accommodate the composting toilets. Instead of using a handle to flush the toilet, we were instructed to put a cup of wood chips, which looked like kitty litter, in the toilet after each use.

The showers were heated by solar heat and supplemented with propane. Lights ran on a battery, which was probably solar-operated. I am ashamed to admit that I had no interest in being environmentally correct. I wanted to stand under warm water and heat myself to the core. The showers are operated with push buttons, but I had a foot of duct tape to hold that button down. The pristine shower room did not have any ventilation, which created a little sauna for me.

After showering, I dressed myself with five layers on top and two on bottom along with two pairs of double lined socks. I even interleaved the tops and bottoms by stuffing the microspore top of the long underwear into the lower half, then the t-shirt into my jeans. In contrast, I put my damp socks and shoes back on, planning to change into dry ones in the tent.

Dan and I returned to the office/store/dining hall to huddle around the store until suppertime.

I wished that Dan could see this room as I had first seen it when Jim and I were here before. Instead of seeming like a cave, the dining hall was bathed in golden sunlight and a soft breeze was slipping in through the screens. The blinds, which were occasionally used to protect diners from evening rains, were rolled up to give us a sweeping view of the meadow while we ate our dinner.

Dan and I reentered the cave and joined the tiny circle at the fire, whose faces were dimly visible. Immediately, we heard

Michelle's twang voice announcing, "My husband is probably sound asleep, because he took his medicine." Looking around, I realized that it was going to be impossible to read in that light. There was enough light to play cards, but it was miserably cold even four feet from the fire.

A couple, Nadine and Neal, interested me. They had hiked in all kinds of places. Nadine had been on a team that prepared an assault on K3 thirty years before. She made me feel less unprepared, when she said, "I have always worn walking shoes and this is the first time that they are inadequate." I recalled the image of Mad Hatter Brian running in his sneakers earlier in the day.

Eventually, we were asked to leave the dining room so that the staff could set up for supper. When I returned to the tent/mess hall, Dan was already seated at a table with our guides. He had gallantly seated himself in the coldest place by the "window." I sat between him and Christy. When Michelle and Ken arrived, they sat across from us. We dined still wearing our coats and hats. The food was delicious but we all agreed that we longed for steaming hot chocolate.

When we were eating our dessert, Brian entered the room, carrying an armload of blankets. He announced, "Quite a few people did not come in today. So, while you were eating, my staff gathered all of the blankets from their beds. Each of you can take a couple more for your own bed."

Adding those blankets to our beds, we each had five layers of wool blankets. We also had our pieces of firewood, kindling and one piece of newspaper, along with printed directions on starting fires in the stove. Even with the directions, we used up our newspaper without getting the wood to ignite. As our newspaper disappeared, I began thinking about the books and papers I had with me. Mom's stories that I was editing came to mind and I offered them to Dan, one page at a time. How would

I tell Mom that her stories had gone up in smoke? I didn't care because we had a roaring fire. We climbed into our beds for the long night. I was fully clothed in multiple layers and an additional pair of wool socks. We both admitted to being quite warm.

But that was only temporary. I can't say I was really cold. I found having my head covered by the blankets helped keep me warm. Dan and I both laughed about how bad our breath smelled when we had to breathe it ourselves.

Occasionally, we heard sleet hitting the tent. I often heard wind sweeping through the tops of pine trees followed by a whoosh on top of our tent. I didn't know if snow was falling off our tent or onto it. During quieter times, I could hear the babble of the stream on Dan's side of the tent. Again, I was puzzled by that sound. Sometimes, I couldn't hear it. Was it because it was overridden by the wind in the trees or did it stop entirely or was it there all along and I wasn't listening for it?

All night long, I contemplated the different sounds, the kinds of snow I had seen and wishing I had words for them. I squeezed myself into a tiny ball trying to conserve my heat. Each time I turned, I carefully tended to my blankets to prevent the seepage of cold air in or my warm air out. There was so little that I could control to make me comfortable. Perhaps, the lesson of this trip lay in this night of searching. My only conclusion was how hard it is to be prepared and how little I can control myself. No great ideas or insights arose from the night. I had had hours and hours all alone and had been free to let my mind wander, and I still was no wiser at the end of the time.

We awoke to a white and frozen world. When we opened our door, we saw that it was still snowing and we couldn't see across the meadow. I knew that if it had been clear, we would have had a magnificent view out our front door. The puddles in front of our tent and on the paths were gone, frozen or covered with snow.

When we went for breakfast, we saw the mules were saddled and had been brought up by the "dining hall." Christy and Dinah came in and sat at the table with Dan and me. Christy said, "We have decided to take you back to the stables. The next part of the trip has lots of cobblestones and could be dangerously slippery, even if the snow stops."

They seemed surprised when Dan replied, "I think that's a good idea. Mom reminded me this morning that tomorrow we'll be going to Vogel sang, which is the highest of the camps. Neither one of us want to be there in this weather."

Christy had borrowed some ski pants for the trip down. We each had more appropriate clothing, so that this time we would not be so cold on the ride. During breakfast, Christy's cowboy hat began to drip into her plate. She kept it on.

Christy made an announcement after breakfast to all the hikers about our plans, saying that the trail might be hard to find in the snow. If anyone wanted to follow the horses, that would muck up the trail for a while and make it easy to find their way back.

We went back and finished packing and dressing for the trip. This time I had a pair of gloves. I also wore a silk undershirt, microspore long underwear (top and bottom) interleaved turtleneck sweater, jeans, winter coat and raincoat. I also was wearing 2 pairs of socks (not wool ones, since they wouldn't fit in my shoes). Dan was also wearing multiple layers. I carried very little for the saddlebags. I had split my duffle bags (dry in waterproof bag and the rest in my nylon duffle bag).

It was still snowing as we filled our water bottles, one of our last acts before leaving. Fortunately, Christy and Dinah had brought our mules up next to the dining hall. Christy says, "I didn't want to walk back to the corral myself; I was worried you would have a hard time getting to it, too."

We got on our mules and readied to leave. I took a few pictures. We tried not to think about how hard it might be driving home.

My mule Cadillac stumbled more often on the trail than the prior day. When we stopped for lunch, I mentioned the stumbling to Christy. She pointed to her horses' hooves, which had about 4 inches of ice under each hoof, and said, "They all have built ups like that. It is hard for them to keep balance." I could see how the ice build-up would make it hard for the animals to walk and I felt chastened. It must be like walking on platform shoes.

It did stop snowing along the way. By the time we were half way to the stables, blue sky could be seen with fluffy clouds. Christy excitedly pointed out Cathedral peaks and told us we would be seeing it from different perspectives on the way home. We actually saw Cathedral Lakes, stopping at an overlook to see them. Just the day before we could only see the edge of one of the lakes.

By the time we stopped at Cathedral Lakes for lunch, the snow had stopped. Everyone was able to get on and off with dignity. The sun popped out on occasion. The snow showed signs of melting on the rocks. We could find a place to sit for lunch.

At lunch, I asked Christy if, having worked a year as a guide, she could tell what people were like fairly quickly. She said, "I have worked other people-oriented jobs and am pretty good at sizing up people. Walker tells us what kinds of people are on our trips. He can really figures out people during the time he has with them. He told me that we would like you two."

Michelle soon joined us, so I couldn't ask any more questions. Ken stayed off by himself.

During the final four miles down, we started meeting hikers out for the day, dressed in light clothes. The snow was melting, and it was hard to believe that a few hours before we had been in a swirling white world with snow covered trees with icicles on their tips. Now, the sky was a perfect deep blue, made even bluer by the contrasting high white clouds. Occasionally, we could see the sweeping vistas that I had remembered longingly. In fact, those views made me feel a lump in my throat and almost made me tear up. Seeing them again made me want them even more.

Christy our guide began to worry what her boss was going to say. At least, she had a few pictures to prove the conditions. When we got within the range of radio signals, Christy heard about one guided group after another coming down. Every one of the horse trips returned to the stables!

After Cathedral Lakes, we started seeing hikers coming up from Tuolumne Meadows. They came in all kinds. Christy said, "They don't have any idea what they are walking into.

One hiker was carrying an umbrella. I heard her tell her companion, "I thought of riding horses like that, but then I wouldn't get any real exercise." We also saw a bare chested hiker. I still had all my layers on and did not feel like shedding any of them. I did notice that Christy had shed her slicker and tied it to the back of her saddle.

The lower we got, the more lightly dressed the hikers were. A family had a baby in a back pack and the child was only wearing a polartec jacket and hat. Having watched the clouds following us and seeing the dark buildup of them behind us, I worried about how the hikers would deal with a sudden weather change.

The boss Walker offered us lodging at Tuoloume Meadows tent cabins and to go on the last leg of our planned trip to Vogelsang on Sunday, stay overnight and return on Monday. Neither Dan nor I could imagine ourselves testing the fates. We had noticed clouds coming in. Truthfully, the guides didn't want to go back either and gave all of the reasons we shouldn't go: higher elevation, still unpredictable weather, no showers, paper plates, limited firewood. We just wanted to go home before the mountain passes snowed closed.

Dan and I went back to Tuolumne Meadows. I cancelled our reservations there and ordered two showers for us. They gave me the towels for free, saying we deserved that break.

During the shower, a camper from Vogelsang talked about how cold it had been up there. She and her husband were the only hikers who stayed in their own tent; all other hikers took advantage of cancellations and moved to the tent cabins. This woman said they were comfortable in their little tent. Being prepared does make a difference.

Another camper was trying to figure out the washcloth trick for keeping the shower on. If I had had more duct tape I would have shared it. It felt so good being bathed in warm water. I did notice that I was not shivering as I undressed and dressed. What a difference a few thousand feet and sunshine warmed air makes.

Showered and a little warmer, Dan and I drove back home, each in our own car.

There was fog in some areas on the Tioga Pass Road. It made me even happier with my decision to go home.

I drove into my garage and entered my house. I heard a key being fit into the front door. It was Dan. He had stopped at our favorite Mexican restaurant El Lorito and bought Carne Asada Burritos for us for supper! Nice warm ending for our Labor Day weekend adventure.

When there is a chance of cold weather, I always carry a pair of gloves.

Ice Skating

Watching children skate at the mall's ice rink, I mused: Something doesn't seem right here. What bothers me about this scene? Why doesn't the ice seem real to me? It looks like ice. It is cold, hard and people are skating on it. Men smooth and polish it with a massive Zamboni machine, like a golf course green is groomed before an important tournament. This rink is a wonder, frozen 365 days a year, unaffected by the weather. These children only need money for admission and a way to get here. But, for me, this rink lacks something. Could it be the romance I associate with ice skating?

I wonder if these people miss it, too. Does the predictability of this place detract or add to their pleasure? Would they enjoy skating out of doors on frozen ponds the way we did? Would they feel the exhilaration that I did skating on satiny ice in the moonlight?

I stopped watching the skaters, took another sip of coffee and settled more comfortably in my seat at the restaurant overlooking the rink. My mind wandered back to the winter of my junior year in high school.

I had lived through sixteen Indiana winters and knew when the pond was about to freeze over. When you walk a quarter of a mile to the bus stop each morning, you develop an intimate awareness of the interplay of the seasons and the weather.

The afternoon of my favorite memory of ice skating, the cold slithered into my coat sleeves, down my neck and up my legs, despite my furry mittens and pink wool scarf. It had been icy cold for the last two days, far too cold for snow. By the time we reached our back door, our cheeks were past rosy and on the verge of cherry red. We opened the kitchen door, tumbled into the warmth and, almost as one, called out, "Mom, we're home. It's cold out there."

"It sure is," Mom replied. "I was watching for the bus, thinking that something warm would feel good to you."

Our noses didn't need to thaw out to smell the freshly popped popcorn filling the chipped crockery bowl on the gray formica kitchen table. Nell checked the oven, sniffed the contents, and smiled back at us.

"Mom warmed tee shirts, jeans and socks for us," she announced. I smiled, too, anticipating the pleasure of donning those warmed garments, knowing that their warmth was going to seep deep into me, like when I basked in bright, warm, gentle spring sunshine.

Reaching into the popcorn bowl, my younger brother Henry asked, "Mom, did Dad check the pond?"

"Yes," she reported, "he went by the pond before dinner, and he thinks it will be ready tomorrow evening—if it stays cold like this for another day. It's already frozen in the shallows, but the deep end still isn't solid enough."

That evening, as soon as Nell heard Dad turning the doorknob to open the back door, she rushed to join him in the unheated mudroom. She gingerly sat herself down on the frigid bench beside Dad. Watching him take his boots off, Nell asked, "Did you check the pond again?" Before he could reply, she continued, "When can we go ice skating?"

My reverie was broken by the waiter offering to refill my coffee cup. Looking at the skaters again, I thought, *They wouldn't understand our concern about the condition of the pond. They skate in a perfectly controlled environment. They have no idea how the caprices of the weather shaped our ice!*

But Dad understood. He knew how much we cherished the few days of good ice.

"I went back to the pond before dark," Dad told Nell. "I think it will be safe for me to test the ice tomorrow, especially if it drops below zero again tonight, like they were predicting on the radio at noon. If there is no breeze to roughen the ice, I think you'll have some good ice out there."

People today would wonder why we asked Dad about the ice, rather than going down to the pond and testing it ourselves. We grew up observing Dad's respect for water and, in turn, respected his safety rules regarding the pond. In the winter, that meant that no one considered venturing onto the pond until Dad, a man who never wore ice skates, tested it and gave it his stamp of approval. As a result, no one ever fell through the ice at our pond, unlike Nell at the horseshoe pond, later that year.

I was pulled back into the present again. I pondered, *Do you think they test the rink's ice? What for? The rink ice is on solid ground. It doesn't need to be an impenetrable barrier between the skaters and fluid, frigid waters. Those skaters never have to fear being trapped beneath an inches-thick lid, wishing they had fallen straight down and could bob back up through the entry hole. I'm glad Dad was so careful.*

I had watched Dad perform this task, so I knew what he planned to do the next day. Dressed in his usual work clothes of overalls, heavy denim coat, gloves, cap and work boots, he would begin the test with a careful step onto the shallow end of the pond, which was only about a foot deep.

With both feet on the ice, he would stamp his foot, listen, and then jump up and down. Standing safely on solid ground nearby, whoever was with him would listen, too, with a muffled sense of dread for any groaning or ripping sound that might signal the cracking of ice. As Dad progressed toward the deep side of the pond, he stopped occasionally to stamp and jump.

Besides raptly listening for an impending disaster, I had also watched his gait. If he shuffled his feet, I wondered, *Is he worried that the ice might break under his weight? Or is the ice so smooth that he is trying to avoid a fall?* If he strode easily across the expanse, a disappointing conclusion began to take root. I concluded, *The ice is rough and crunchy. It's going to grab our skates and turn them into ice walkers. We are going to look and feel like we are wearing skinny snowshoes.*

Dad's thorough examination of the pond was sometimes frustrating. How long can a kid remain patient while watching her Dad jumping up and down, listening and peering into the ice? We sometimes resorted to teasing him, "Do you have to drive a tractor onto the pond to prove that the ice is ready?"

That night, when we dressed for bed in our drafty, cold second-story bedroom, nobody complained about the chilled bed clothes or the long icy fingers of cold air slithering into bed with us. We just said the words, "ice skating," smiled, and snuggled closer to each other. I said a little prayer asking for perfect weather conditions—a cold, still night to produce hard, smooth ice tomorrow.

I had seen promising ice turn into a skater's nightmare before. We knew that a breeze could stir the water and keep it from making ice crystals, or just as bad, make it freeze with a skin of bumpy warts.

Fortunately, it was too cold to snow that night. Snow and ice skating do not mix. We had tried shoveling paths for skating before and found ice is fused to the snow. At best, the path had a crackling off-white frosting conducive to ice marching, not ice skating. A similar crust sometimes developed when the top inch of ice melted and froze again. Patches of crusty ice can send the unwary ice skater sprawling onto the ice—a situation that never would occur at an ice rink.

The next morning, when we came down for breakfast, the smell of smoked sausage and Dad was waiting for us. "I thought you would like to know I looked at the pond this morning after I fed the livestock. It looks smooth, and it's solid. I'll check it before you get home from school and put the kerosene stove by the pond for you. You can plan on skating there this afternoon."

Mom scraped the fried potatoes into a bowl, handed it to me to place on the table and said, "Janie, you said something about wanting to ask Ann Eddleman to skate. There is going to be a full moon tonight, so you can go skating after dark, too. Today at school, why don't you ask her if she would like to come over this evening? I'll pick her up after supper, about six o'clock."

Then, she handed a steaming bowl of milk gravy to Nell and said, "Do you want to invite Kay? Or Pam? I might as well pick them up when I get Ann."

Walking to the bus stop, we didn't complain about the cold. Instead, we excitedly discussed our plans for the afternoon and evening.

That afternoon, we practically ran home from the bus stop. Before we could pop out the question, Mom had the answer, "You can go skating."

Too excited to look for snacks or warming clothes, we ran to our bedrooms and started putting on layers of clothes—nylon stockings, two layers of socks, jeans, tee shirt or blouse, flannel shirt, sweater, coat, mittens and hat. Within ten minutes, we were back in the mudroom putting on our boots. Together, Nell, Henry, Bet and I walked down to the pond with our skates slung over our shoulders.

The first ice of the year gleamed in the sunlight and beckoned us.

"Br-r-r! It is cold!" Nell exclaimed, as she sat on the hard icy-cold snow at the pond's edge to change into her ice skates.

She looked at the stove and asked, "Henry, will you light this for us?"

"No," Henry replied, "it will only make the ground mushy. Let's skate a while. There's no breeze; I bet we get warmed up. If not, I'll light the stove for you."

"I wish it didn't have to be so cold to make ice," Nell complained. "I can't believe my foot feels the cold as soon as I take my shoe off."

"It's the moisture in your socks. It's freezing," I noted. My tendency to think scientifically was not appreciated by my younger sister. I continued, "Wait until you put your foot inside your skate. I bet it sends a shiver right up to your shoulders when you do it!"

Like a research subject, Nell responded to the suggestion. "Br-r-r!" she said, and, shivering, she slipped her foot in an ice skate.

"Look at my fingers," she said, showing us her red hands. "It hurts my fingers to pull these laces."

Despite her complaints, Nell was the first on the ice. She looked back at us and grinned; the cold was forgotten.

Shortly, all four of us began to get our skating legs back. The first white squiggles traced by our skates on the ice soon became confident long strokes. Still, there were occasional falls.

"Wow! This ice is so smooth. Doesn't it feel as if we are floating on a tiny beads of air?" I called to the others.

Our sense of freedom increased as activity warmed us and we began shedding our outer layers of stiff padding. Skating across the icy expanse, I relished the feeling of being released from the rules of nature. Foot stepping gravity gave way to smooth stretched out glides. The cold couldn't penetrate the aura of warmth produced by our muscles. Our worries were left at the pond's edge. The ice was a little bit of heaven on earth.

Too soon, we heard the car horn's "Beeeeeeep. Beeeeeeep. Beep. Beep," which was Mom's signal that it was time to return home.

Noticing a pager on skater's belt and a cell phone on another's, I thought, Mom's car horn signals probably would be considered in the same category as drumming or smoke signals by these technology-oriented people.

We quickly readied ourselves for the walk back home. The shoes didn't feel as cold as the ice skates had earlier. Ice skates over our shoulders and arms loaded with our unneeded outer clothing, we turned our backs to the pond and went home for supper.

After supper, Mom said, "Janie and Nell, you don't have to do dishes tonight. Come with me to pick up Ann and Kay." The other kids glared at us. The perfect day had gotten even better!

When Mom dropped us off at the pond, the fire was already glowing in the stove, its chimney looking like a candle planted on snowy-white frosting. The snowy ground glittered and the ice echoed the flickering flames. The radiant warmth promised respite from the cold.

Putting on our skates was a pleasure, rather than an ordeal. At Mom's suggestion, during the drive from town, we had put our ice skates near the heater's warm duct. Donning the skates was like wrapping my feet in soft oven-warmed clothes.

As I put on my skates, I periodically admired our surroundings. In the moonlight, the ice looked like black satin with bits of white lace offset by glowing jewels from the fire. A myriad of stars winked through the wispy pink hints of the aurora borealis. Dark gray cedars drooped at the shallow end of the pond and the nearby bare maples raised their limbs towards the stars.

Will be able to shed these heavy coats, like we did this afternoon?" I thought, launching myself out onto the ice.

The night wrapped its dreamy mood around me. By the moon's light, I could see the marks our skates had scrawled in the ice earlier in the day. Each skater was accompanied by a mimicking moon shadow. The ethereal self held the skater to the ice, but, like a dance partner, moved in a shared rhythm. In the half-light, our movements seemed languid and graceful, as if in slow motion. The mood was deepened by the muffled laughter and hushed conversations.

With regret, we stopped skating at nine o'clock, as Mom had directed us. We walked home through the maple grove. The moon lit the way and decorated the ground with a cobweb of shadows from the bare branches overhead.

When we opened the kitchen door, the yeasty smell of fresh bread greeted us. A hot-from-the-oven Golden Crown coffee cake studded with pecans and oozing a thick glistening cinnamon syrup was in the middle of the kitchen table.

Mom smiled and said, "Sit down and eat while the bread's hot." Reaching for a pot, she continued, "I'll make you some hot chocolate."

In the warm kitchen, sipping hot chocolate, eating homemade fresh-baked sweet bread, chatting with my friend and surrounded by a caring family, it was the perfect ending for an idyllic day.

Hot, Hot, Hot

The day was going to be a "scorcher." I awakened at daybreak. My bedcovers were flung off and I still felt warm. The bed sheets under me clung to my skin. Hair damp at the roots. A thin patina of moisture all over my body.

On scorcher days, the locusts started their incessant high-pitched squealing soon after sunrise. But, on really hot days, even the locusts stopped calling for a mate by noon.. They wouldn't resume their droning until sunset neared. How I wished my parents would copy the locusts' schedule for the farm work!

Indiana's steaming soup promoted fecundity. Moisture rose from the ground and hung on the horizon like steam rising from a simmering soup pot. Corn leaves pointed up and grew into the sky, while the ears on either side of the stalk filled, grew heavy, then drooped with their weight of golden nuggets. Grass grew inches every day. Mom's vegetable garden produced mounds of beans, corn, and tomatoes that had to be preserved. Blackberries bulged with sweet dark purple juice.

Unfortunately, the same conditions that nurtured our food supply also encouraged pesky bugs. Flies polka dotted our porch and clung to the screen door. Mosquitoes whined around sitting targets. Anyone foolhardy enough to sleep without a light covering would have itching welts for a week. Imagine what the mosquitoes would do with anyone who dared to sleep out of doors at night! Chiggers slipped unseen up pant legs and settled into skin folds in the groin and armpits and along belt lines to drive their victims mad with unremitting itching that was exacerbated by heat and moisture. Colonies of bees and wasps seemed to multiply exponentially. The warm moisture that made me feel like I was slogging through mud was the perfect media for insect reproduction and growth.

I contributed to the moisture content. It oozed from my body with any exertion. It poured out when I helped cook meals or hoed in the garden. Sweat trickled down my nose and off my elbows. It dampened my shirt. The hairline above my brow became wet and the tendrils at my neckline grew darker and curlier. Even when I sat still, beads of sweat outlined my brow.

We tried to do the sweatiest jobs in the morning while the cool dew was still on the grass. Trails of flattened, darker-green grass spread out to the garden, the chicken house, the clothesline, and to the lane. Our bare feet relished the watery coolness of the silver-tinged grass and etched paths on our way to chores. When we picked the beans and other vegetables before the locusts began their squiry song, the night's chilly condensation washed our limbs. Although stiffer weeds were easier to chop with a sickle later in the day, we preferred to slug away at flaccid stocks and be sprayed by their dew. We knew that sun would soon transform those cooling droplets into a muggy haze.

There was no escaping the steam of the kitchen though. It rose from the meals we cooked and hung in the room. Yet, when the men came in at noon from the sun's sizzling cauldron, they would look at the steaming food on the table and tell us how comfortable it felt in the kitchen. Savoring their food, they wouldn't notice the dishpans full of tomatoes or green beans we had picked in the dewy morning. They wouldn't understand my dread of the impending ordeal.

To keep the kitchen "comfortable" for the noon meal, Mom had saved the canning for the afternoon. While the men ate, I mentally positioned myself for picnic table duty. I would volunteer to supervise my younger siblings in washing and otherwise preparing the produce outside at the picnic table, where there was, at least, a chance of a cooling breeze. But, being the oldest, I knew I probably be assigned to kitchen duty. Inside there, I preferred to inspect the quality of the prepared produce and plant it in superheated jars. If I had to put the jars into the simmering water bath, the rising vapors added to the sweat already on my face and upper arms. At least, those were short assaults of steamy heat. Worse was having to squeeze juice out of steaming stewed tomatoes. I would be making my own stifling sauna as I spooned seething tomato pulp into a strainer and turned its handle to make juice dribble down into the pot, which exhaled tomato juice vapors.

During free time, we kids searched for relief from the stifling heat. Playing with the Ewing children meant that we could luxuriate in their house, which had thick walls to fortify it from onslaughts of the surrounding heat. Its basement was cooler still. In desperation, we once tried sitting in the dark on the bottom step of our musty cellar. These cool comforts were short-lived. Although these places felt cool when we entered them, our bodies quickly acclimated to the new surroundings and we began to feel hot there, too.

Moving air offered a better reprieve. We waved handheld fans, sat on stool fans and stood in front of oscillating fans. Best of all was standing in front of the attic door. The 36" blades of giant grain-drying fan Dad had installed in the attic window sucked air from open windows and doors through the house past the attic door and out the little attic window. At night, when only a few windows were open, I vied to sleep near one of those windows.

The only way hot, hot, hot weather could be endured was to hope for a cooling rain. Then the hot, hot, hot weather would be reduced to hot weather.

Barefoot

I am a child of the soil. These wide flat feet came from generations of people who trod upon clods of dirt. We feel the pulse of the earth through the soles of our feet.

My feet loved the summer the best. Shoes were shed except for a few hours on Sundays. Free of coverings, they communicated vivid descriptions of the world. My eyes could see that the green grass was newly mown and my nose smelled the broken aroma that hovered in the air. My bare feet sensed the distinctive feel of the shorn blades. Like a thick oriental carpet, the new mown grass could be rocked underfoot. In a few days, that even-cut turf would become tall enough for me to slice through the grass with my feet, feeling the blades finger my ankles.

Walking through our thick lawn, juicy with morning dew tickled my soul. The softness of the dawn and the sounds of the night critters clung to the cool silkiness of the droplets. It was as if the grass had charmed the humidity from the air in the darkness and threaded its beads onto the blades. I delighted in swishing my feet through dew-laden grass and flinging the many-hued jewels in all directions.

A few hours later, I would bathe my feet in sun-warmed dust puddles, places where rain had collected in footpaths, dried up and left behind a fluffy powder of silty soil as soft as talcum powder. It felt softer than the ostrich feather on Nell's Easter bonnet, softer than Mom's powder puff. They begged me to slow down and pat, pat my soles and wiggle my toes – to let their luxurious velvetiness rise up through my soles to be embedded in my soul.

When my feet were released each summer, they tasted the world anew. They sipped the coolness of the water gushing in bursts from the pump's spout. They sank in the freshly tilled earth between the rows of vegetables. When I approached the young maple tree in our back yard, my feet would tingle in anticipation as I wrapped my arms around the waist-thick limb protruding from the trunk just inches above my head. Then, my feet would make a perpendicular walk up the prickly bark until my legs could wrap around the limb and then propel me to a sitting position in the tree. These pleasures were repeated year after year.

Each year, I dreaded the "lane dance" at the beginning of bare foot season. We kids would gingerly tiptoe onto the center of the lane, where the limestone rocks had not been beaten down by tires, then dare each other to run along the ridge. The jagged rocks stabbed and jabbed our footpads. Uncontrollably, our feet would jump up, first one, and then the other, like the cowboys on television trying to avoid the bullets aimed at their boots. No matter how hard we tried to flatten our feet on those rocks, they twitched up. After a week or so, the teeth of the sharp rocks and cinders had stopped biting. The rocks in the lane were tamed! We could walk on them without cries of "Pain. Pain!" being sent to our brains. My feet could still sense single blades of grass, the squishiness of dirt and the temperature changes from shade to sun, but the rocks no longer stabbed or jabbed.

And so the cycles were repeated each year with my feet being released at the beginning of summer to receive a burst of sensory impressions that were haphazardly preserved. The season of feasting ended with confinement in new school shoes.

Years later, on good days, I found that writing can be like a bare foot summer. I toss aside the insulating layers of cultural, religious and educational injunctions, dig my toes into primordial feelings and memories of my childhood. Eyes closed, I walk through that landscape once again and send snapshots through my fingertips to this paper.

I am a child of the soil who has grown into a woman who harvests words.

AFTERWORD

"You must always remember to check below
the layers of things to find the truth,"
Uncle Jiro explained to Pearl Diver that Mt. Fuji
covers two older volcanos
(*The Pearl Diver* by Jeff Talarigo)

Threads Running Through My Life

This is the end of my book and it's time for me to answer the question I asked Mom while we were working on her memoir, "Do you see any themes in your life?" I have been tossing it around for years. It's even harder to answer than deciding what I wanted in my self-portrait.

Finishing this manuscript on Thanksgiving Day helped me put the question into perspective. The threads that run through my life are:

- gratitude for getting to live the life I am living,
- an understanding that the meaning of an event in my life can change, especially if viewed with compassion,
- the blessings of being surrounded by a loving family and friends.

My life is like a faceted stone.

My friend Lyle transforms rough dingy stones into sparkling gems with his art of faceting.

Faceting is the shaping of a gemstone into a jewel with many sides, or facets. Before Lyle begins to work on a stone, he studies it and considers which pattern would best bring out the beauty of the stone. Then, he carefully plots how to execute that pattern and, finally, meticulously facets it.

I think each of us comes in this world like one of Lyle's semiprecious stones. Life tosses us and turns us, rubbing off the rough edges, shaping and polishing us. Our life experiences gradually turn us into multifaceted people. Someday, hopefully, we'll be like a perfectly faceted gem, showing off the charm of our inner nature.

When you ask people who know a person to tell you about him, each of them might tell you something different, because each person would be speaking from his or her perspective. But, if you listen to all the stories and consider them lovingly, you'll see the beauty of the gem the person has become.

Writing is like faceting. I hold up a story and try to describe what I see, hear, feel, smell and taste. I think about each story, turn it over and look at it from various angles, hoping to hone it to show its inner truth. Then, I write and edit.

I'm done editing this book, but have more stories to facet.

Little Girl, Where Are You?

Little girl with curly blonde hair
Are you still there?

Barefoot adventurer, oh, so small,
Do you still travel now that you are tall?

Teary-eyed youngster, taken aside
When the Santa myth died, why did you hide?

Big sister, working each day,
How did you forget to play?

Outraged teen, History queen,
Why did you let truth go unseen?

Compliant helper, lessons learned well,
Your wishes lay buried. Why didn't you tell?

Lover, Wife-to-be, voice unburied,
You said, "I will be married!"

Mother. Teacher. Nurse. Wife.
Honest, responsible, worker. For life?

Weeping Widow, wipe you tears.
Look beyond your fears.

Now is the time. Don't fear.
Rediscover the child God sent here.

Blonde hair turned to gray,
It's time for you to play.

Little girl with curly blonde hair
Come out, come out, if you dare

Your voice is waiting to be set free.
But, first, you have to laugh joyfully.

Little girl with curly blonde hair,
You are cherished. I care.